Take the Power to Change the World
globalisation and the debate on power

Cover photo:
Rally in Lille, France, 2007

Socialist Resistance would be glad to have readers' opinions of this book, and any suggestions you may have for future publications or wider distribution.

Socialist Resistance books are available at special quantity discounts to educational and non-profit organizations, and to bookstores.

To contact us, please write to:
Socialist Resistance, PO Box 1109, London N4 2UU, Britain
or email us at:
contact@socialistresistance.net
or visit: www.socialistresistance.net

Designed by Ed Fredenburgh
Published June 2007 jointly by Socialist Resistance and the International Institute for Research and Education (IIRE) as IIRE Notebook for Study and Research 37

Printed in Britain by Lightning Source
ISBN: 978-0-902869-94-3
EAN: 9780902869943
ISSN: 0298-7899

TAKE THE POWER TO CHANGE THE WORLD

globalisation and the debate on power

Edited with an introduction by Phil Hearse

Notes on Contributors:

John Holloway, a founding editor of Capital and Class, formerly taught at Edinburgh University and now teaches at the Institute for Humanities and Social Sciences at the Autonomous University of Puebla, Mexico.

Daniel Bensaïd was a leading figure in the French 'events' of 1968. A long-time leader of the Ligue Communiste Révolutionnaire, he is the author of more than 20 books, including Marx for our Time (Verso, 2003). He teaches Philosophy at the University of Paris-VIII.

4

Michael Löwy is a well-known Marxist theorist. He is the author of numerous books, including in English The Politics of Uneven Development – Permanent Revolution Today and Fatherland or Mother Earth on the national question. A research director at the National Centre for Scientific Research in Paris, he is a member of the Ligue Communiste Révolutionnaire.

M Junaid Alam wrote his article in 2005 when he was co-editor of the radical youth journal Left Hook and a student at Northeastern University. His article is reprinted from Seven Oaks magazine.

Phil Hearse has been active in far-left poilitics for more than 40 years and is an editor of the online magazine International Viewpoint.

Contents

Introduction:
Towards a new international left?

On 1 January 1994, 3,000 members of Zapatista Army of National Liberation (EZLN) seized six towns and hundreds of ranches in Chiapas, south eastern Mexico. The uprising was timed to coincide with the implementation of the North American Free Trade Agreement (NAFTA) which the Zapatistas called a 'death sentence' for indigenous peoples. The agreement necessitated changes to Article 27 of the Mexican Constitution, ending the *ejido* system of nationalised land and collective peasant agriculture, so that land could now be sold to international agribusiness. This directly challenged the ability of Mexican farmers to earn a living against powerful US-based agribusiness interests. The rebels directed their uprising toward control of their local communities and the achievement of ten essential goals: work, land, housing, food, health care, education, independence, freedom, democracy, justice, and peace.

This rebellion marked the beginning of an international fightback against neoliberal globalisation, itself propelled by the massive defeats – material, ideological and political – that the left and working class movements suffered in the 1980s and 1990s. It helped generate a significant global justice movement that burst onto the scene dramatically in protests at the founding conference of the World Trade Organisation at the end of November 1999. Estimates ranged from 50,000 to 100,000 protestors.

Protesters came from all over the world, not just the developed countries. They ranged from human rights groups, students, environmental groups, labour rights and trade union activists and the militant Left, all wanting fairer trade without exploitation. In the pouring rain, the Seattle police cracked down viciously on the demonstrators, thus inadvertently dramatising the protests, which caused media headlines worldwide.

The Zapatista rebels and the Seattle demonstrators were the tip of an iceberg of social and political revolt against the injustices of corporate-led globalisation. What followed was the development of the international Social Forum movement. The first World Social Forum was held in 2001 in Porto Alegre, Brazil with some 20,000 people attending. World Social Forums have been held each year since then. There were 150,000 at the 2005 Forum, also held in Porto Alegre and in tens of thousands at 2006 'polycentric' forums are being held in Caracas, Venezuela; Bamako, Mali; and Karachi, Pakistan.

Since the first Word Social Forum, there have been dozens of regional, national and city based forums. The development of the global justice movement itself provided a springboard for the growth of the anti-war movement, which on February 15 2002 brought millions onto the streets worldwide in an attempt to stop the US-led coalition's brutal war on Iraq, which started on 20 March that year.

This panorama of radical developments disproved almost immediately the End of History theories of Francis Fukuyama,[1] who interpreted the fall of the Berlin Wall and the Soviet Union as a definite end of the Left and anti-capitalist radicalism and a final victory of liberal-democratic capitalism, which would never again be challenged. A great ferment of anti-corporate and anti-capitalist movements and ideas spread internationally, spurred by the colonisation of the Internet by global justice campaigners. Just a decade after the 'end of history', history decided to get going again.

It was against this background that Irish academic John Holloway, working in Puebla, Mexico, came forward with his 2002 book *Change the World without Taking Power* (Pluto Press). The book took up a phrase used by Zapatista leader Subcommandante Marcos, that the EZLN wanted to democratise Mexico, but did not seek to "take power". The very success of Holloway's book, the fact that it was taken the least bit seriously, came from the political conjuncture – the 'spirit of the times'. For tens of thousands of global justice and anti-war activists, often influenced by the ideas of NGOs,[2] the aim was precisely to make the world fairer and curb the power of the multinational corporations, but not necessarily to end capitalism as such. Even among conscious anti-capitalists, the political party form, and the idea of any type of left-wing government was discredited.

The political character of the new radicalisation at the dawn of a new millennium was indeed influenced by the decline of working class labour movements and the apparent 'failure' of socialism, as shown by the collapse of the Soviet Union and the other Stalinist states. As the working class was less and less a militant political pole in society, millions of young people in the West reached adulthood without any direct knowledge of the trade unions and the political left. The apparent defeat of socialism opened the way to less structured and coherent forms of radicalism. As supporters of Socialist Resistance in Britain put it, the radicalisation was very broad, but not every deep. This is demonstrated by a strange paradox; the anti-war movement in Britain had at its heart the Stop the War Coalition, which in turn was led by the Socialist Workers Party (SWP). But despite two million people on the streets in February 2003, the SWP hardly grew in this period.

This is an extraordinary paradox compared with the late 1960s. Then, the Vietnam Solidarity Campaign never mobilised more than 100,000 demonstrators – a pretty run-of-the-mill size of demo for the Stop the War coalition. But in late '60s, the period of the Vietnamese revolution and working class advance and not retreat in Europe, every left-wing organisation grew. Political consciousness was much more open to socialism and Marxism in various forms, and indeed the European revolutionary left was ideologically and organisationally reborn in this period.

Holloway's book was greeted by a barrage of left-wing criticism, which among revolutionary Marxists was initiated by my 2003 review of his book, reproduced below. Marxists from the Trotskyist tradition felt particularly aggrieved by the book, because it seemed to attribute to all leftists the same concept of an authoritarian state characteristic of the Stalinists and social democrats. In addition, the book seemed almost politically autistic in the face of Marxist arguments about the necessity to crush the power of the capitalists and their state, and replace both by people's power, workers power, as the alternative framework needed to grow alternative, non-exploitative, social relations.

In politics even highly abstract theoretical debates are rarely resolved on paper, but usually – insofar as they are relevant – by the test of practice. The final test of practice of the Holloway thesis will not of course come until the world has gone beyond capitalism. But since the year 2000 a whole new series of experiences have put the Holloway thesis to the test. First and foremost have been the massive anti-neoliberal struggles in Latin America, and most significantly the emergence of the left-wing governments of Hugo Chávez in Venezuela and Evo Morales in Bolivia, now followed by Rafael Correa in Ecuador. In these countries there is no serious argument on the left that these government should not exist or should resign: rather the debate is about what concrete steps these governments should take, and what their relationship to the mass movement and the popular masses in general should be. Interviewing Holloway in April 2005, American radical John Ross noted: "John Holloway's thesis is not much endorsed by Latin American left leaders who are closest to taking power. 'What an absurd idea! We are fighting to take state power because we want to change things. How else can you make these changes?' exclaims Evo Morales, leader of

Bolivia's coca farmers and the Movement Towards Socialism which is only a hairsbreadth away from the presidency of his country."[3]

Whatever the eventual outcome in Bolivia and Venezuela, the very existence of governments that claim to be socialist is of huge ideological significance internationally. In Bolivia the Morales MAS[4] government is the product of huge struggles over control of the country's gas, oil and water supplies that generated massive social movements. You could say that the social movements created the MAS government. By contrast the mammoth social eruption in Argentina in 2001-3 after the collapse of the currency, which saw both the Argentinean state and that country's capitalist class on the verge of collapse and millions of people mobilised in vast social movements, did not lead to the creation of a left-wing government. An historical opportunity for the working class has been lost. James Petras describes the reasons for this thus:

"What emerges from the extended and massive popular rebellion is that spontaneous uprising are not a substitute for political power... What clearly was lacking was a unified political organization (party, movement or combination of both) with roots in the popular neighborhoods which was capable of creating representative organs to promote class-consciousness and point toward taking state power. As massive and sustained as was the initial rebellious period (December 2001-July 2002) no such political party or movement emerged – instead a multiplicity of localized groups with different agendas soon fell to quarreling over an elusive "hegemony" – driving millions of possible supporters toward local face-to-face groups devoid of any political perspective. Clearly the slogan "Que se vayan todos" (Out with all politicians) which circulated widely among those recently engaged in struggle, turned out to be counterproductive as it further delayed or short-circuited the necessary political education which an emerging political leadership required to deepened long-term mass engagement in revolutionary politics."[5]

The events in Argentina are a decisive rejection of the idea of that local and 'autonomous' rebellion, without being linked up nationally and internationally into a coherent political project to take power, can decisively 'change the world'.

If anti-capitalist radicalisation has grown in the first decade of the new century, and without the Left has found new wind in its sails, new experiences are maturing, clarifying and recomposing that Left. It is now clear that a section of the international Left that grew and found support by its decisive rejection of neoliberalism and the new era of imperialist mega-violence, has ended up accommodating itself to it. A tragic case of the Workers Party (PT)-led government of Lula in Brazil. Lula's government, far from bringing about radical social reform, has had a minimal impact on the lives of the poor or the privileges of the rich in one of the most unequal countries on Earth. This has directly led to the split in the PT, to form the PSOL – Party of Socialism and Liberty, to maintain the class struggle and anti-capitalist traditions of the old PT.

In Italy in the first years of the decade *Rifondazione Comunista* (Communist Refoundation party) – the militant wing of the old Italian Communist party – made a decisive shift to the left and championed the global justice movement. The European Social Forum in Florence in 2002 marked the high point of the party's radicalism. Subsequently however, under the pressure of the 'centre-left' and the perceived need to do make any alliance at all to defeat Silvio Berlusconi, the party has become part of the centre-left Prodi government's coalition and voted for the war in Afghanistan. This has been resisted notably by the *Sinistra Critica* (Critical Left) current.[6]

The question of what attitude to take towards participation in a possible 'social-liberal' or French 'Blairite' government has also been at the centre of debates and disputes in the radical French Left. In April 2007 the influential Revolutionary Communist league (LCR) refused to put up a joint candidate with the Communist Party, who wanted to continue their old practice of taking seats in social democratic or centre-left governments. This decision was arguably vindicated by the powerful election campaign of the LCR's presidential candidate Olivier Besancenot, who scored more than double the votes of the Communist candidate Marie-George Buffet.

In any case, the developments in Latin America, the division in the Brazilian PT, the Left clashes in Italy and France – all these things constitute what Daniel Bensaïd calls in an article published below as *The Return of Strategy*. Bensaïd characterises the early period of the global justice movement when Holloway published his book as a 'utopian moment':

"Simplifying somewhat, I call this the 'utopian moment' of social movements, which took different forms: utopias based on the regulation of free markets; Keynesian utopias; and above all neo-libertarian utopias, in which the world can be changed without taking power or by making do with counter-powers (John Holloway, Toni Negri, Richard Day).... This 'return of politics' has led to a revival in debates about strategy. Witness the polemics round the books of Holloway, Negri and Michael Albert, and the differing appraisals of the Venezuelan process and of Lula's administration in Brazil.... We are coming to the end of the phase of the big refusal and of stoical resistance – Holloway's 'scream' in the face of 'the mutilation of human lives by capitalism', slogans like 'The world is not a commodity' or 'Our world is not for sale'. We need to be specific about what the 'possible' world is and, above all, to explore how to get there."

Subcommandante Marcos in April 2007, announcing the second phase of the 'Other Campaign', said "Another world is possible, but only on top of the corpse of capitalism". Exactly so. Another world is possible but only on the basis of revolution, the destruction of their power and the creation of ours. Not for nothing is Victor Serge's book entitled The Birth of Our Power. When working people move to destroy the capitalist system they will of course base themselves on a huge web of self-organisation and social movements, as well as socialist political parties. But the self-organisation of the masses will need to be co-ordinated into a functioning system of self-organised, bottom-up administration. Our power.

Phil Hearse, 6 May 2007

Notes

1 Frances Fukuyama: The End of History and The Last Man (1992)

2 See James Petras: A Marxist Critique of Post-Marxists at Links magazine: http://www.dsp.org.au/links/back/issue09/petras.htm

3 John Ross: How to Change the World without Taking Power, Counterpunch magazine: http://www.counterpunch.org/ross04022005.html

4 Movimiento al Socialismo – Movement Towards Socialism

5 James Patras: Argentina – From Popular Rebellion to 'Normal' Capitalism: http://www.marxsite.com/petrasargentina.pdf

6 See A New Period for the Italian Left, Franco Turigliatto and Salvatore Cannavò http://www.internationalviewpoint.org/spip.php?article1255

John Holloway
Twelve theses on changing the world without taking power

2004

1 The starting point is negativity.

We start from the scream, not from the word. Faced with the mutilation of human lives by capitalism, a scream of sadness, a scream of horror, a scream of anger, a scream of refusal: NO.

Thought, to be true to the scream, must be negative. We do not want to understand the world, but to negate it. The aim of theorising is to conceptualise the world negatively, not as something separate from practice, but as a moment of practice, as part of the struggle to change the world, to make it a place fit for humans to live in.

But how, after all that has happened, can we even begin to think of changing the world?

2 A world worthy of humanity cannot be created through the state.

For most of the last century, efforts to create a world worthy of humanity were focussed on the state and the winning of state power. The main controversies (between 'reformists' and 'revolutionaries') were about how to win state power, whether by parliamentary or by extra-parliamentary means. The history of the twentieth century suggests that the question of how to win state power was not very important. In all cases, the winning of state power failed to bring about the changes that the militants hoped for. Neither reformist nor revolutionary governments succeeded in radically changing the world.

It is easy to accuse all the leaderships of these movements of 'betraying' the movements which they led. So many betrayals suggest, however, that the failure of radical, socialist or communist governments lies much deeper. The reason that the state cannot be used to bring about radical change in society is that the state itself is a form of social relations that is embedded in the totality of capitalist social relations. The very existence of the state as an instance separated from society means that, whatever the contents of its policies, it takes part actively in the process of separating people from control of their own lives. Capitalism is simply that: the separating of people from their own doing. A politics that is oriented towards the state inevitably reproduces within itself the same process of separating: separating leaders from led, serious political activity from frivolous personal activity. A politics oriented towards the state, far from bringing about a radical change in society, leads to the progressive subordination of opposition to the logic of capitalism.

We can see now that the idea that the world could be changed through the state was an illusion. We are fortunate enough to be living the end of that illusion.

3 The only way in which radical change can be conceived today is not as the taking of power but as the dissolution of power.

Revolution is more urgent than ever. The horrors arising from the capitalist organisation of society are becoming more and more intense. If revolution through the winning of state power has proved to be an illusion, this does not mean that we should abandon the question of revolution. But we must think of it in other terms: not as the taking of power, but as the dissolution of power.

4 The struggle for the dissolution of power is the struggle for the emancipation of power-to (potentia) from power-over (potestas).

To even think of changing society without taking power, we must make a distinction between power-to (potentia) and power-over (potestas).

Any attempt to change society involves doing, activity. Doing, in turn, implies that we have the capacity to do, the power-to-do. We often use 'power' in this sense, as something good, as when a united action with others (a demonstration or even a good seminar) makes us feel 'powerful'. Power in this sense is rooted in doing: it is power-to-do.

Power-to-do is always social, always part of a social flow of doing. Our ability to do is produced by the doing of others and creates the conditions for the future doing of others. It is impossible to imagine a doing that does not integrate in some way with the doing of others, past, present or future.

5 Power-to is transformed into power-over when doing is broken.

The transformation of power-to into power-over implies the breaking of the social flow of doing. Those who exercise power-over separate the done from the doing of others and declare it to be theirs. The appropriation of the done is at the same time the appropriation of the means of doing, and this allows the powerful to control the doing of the doers. The doers (humans, understood as active) are thus separated from their done, from the means of doing and from doing itself. As doers, they are separated from themselves. This separation, which is the basis of any society in which some exercise power over others, reaches its highest point in capitalism.

The social flow of doing is broken. Power-to is transformed into power-over. Those who control the doing of others now appear as the Doers of society, and those whose doing is controlled by others become invisible, without face, without voice. Power-to-do no longer appears to be part of a social flow, but exists in the form of an individual power. For most people the power-to-do things becomes transformed into its opposite, powerlessness, or, at most, the power-to-do things determined by others. For the powerful, power-to-do becomes transformed into power-over, the power to tell others what to do, and therefore a dependence upon the doing of others.

In present society, power-to exists in the form of its own negation, as power-over. Power-to exists in the mode of being denied. This does not mean that it ceases to exist. It exists, but it exists as denied, in antagonistic tension to its own form of existence as power-over.

6 The breaking of doing is the breaking of every aspect of society, every aspect of ourselves.

The separation of the done from the doing and from the doers means that people relate to one another no longer as doers, but as owners (or non-owners) of the done (seen now as a thing divorced from doing). Relations between people exist as relations between things, and people no longer exist as doers but as the passive bearers of things.

This separation of doers from doing and hence from themselves is variously referred to in the literature as alienation (the young Marx), fetishism (the older Marx), reification (Lukács), discipline (Foucault) or identification (Adorno). All of these terms make it clear that power-over cannot be understood as something external to us, but that it reaches into every aspect of our existence. All of these terms point to a rigidification of life, a damming of the social flow of doing, a closure of possibilities.

Doing is converted into being: this is the core of power-over. Whereas doing means that we are and are not, the breaking of doing means that the 'and are not' is torn away. We are left just with 'we are': identification. 'We are not' is either forgotten or treated as mere dreaming. Possibility is torn from us. Time is homogenised. The future is now the extension of the present, the past the preparation for the present. All doing, all movement, is contained within the extension of what is. It might be nice to dream of a world worthy of humanity, but that is just a dream: this is the way things are. The rule of power-over is the rule of 'that is the way things are', the rule of identity.

7 We participate in the breaking of our own doing, the construction of our own subordination.

As doers separated from our own doing, we re-create our own subordination. As workers we produce the capital that subordinates us. As university teachers, we play an active part in the identification of society, in the transformation of doing into being. When we define, classify or quantify, or when we hold that the aim of science is to understand society as it is, or when we pretend to study society objectively, as though it were an object separate from us, we actively participate in the negation of doing, in the separation of subject and object, in the divorcing of doer from done.

8 There is no symmetry between power–to and power–over.

Power-over is the breaking and negation of doing. It is the active and repeated negation of the social flow of doing, of the we who constitute ourselves through social doing. To think that the conquest of power-over can lead to the emancipation of that which it negates is absurd.

Power-to is social. It is the constitution of the 'we', the practice of the mutual recognition of dignity.

The movement of power-to against power-over should not be conceived as counter-power (a term which suggests a symmetry between power and counter-power) but rather as anti-power (a term which, for me, a complete a-symmetry between power and our struggle).

9 **Power-over appears to penetrate us so deeply that the only possible solution seems to be the intervention of a force from outside. This is no solution at all.**

It is not difficult to reach highly pessimistic conclusions about present society. The injustices and the violence and the exploitation scream at us, and yet there seems to be no possible way out. Power-over seems to penetrate every aspect of our lives so deeply that it is hard to imagine the 'revolutionary masses' once dreamed of. In the past, the deep penetration of capitalist domination led many to see the solution in terms of the leadership of a vanguard party, but this proved to be no solution at all, as it simply replaced one form of power-over with another.

The easiest answer is pessimistic disillusion. The initial scream of rage at the horrors of capitalism is not abandoned, but we learn to live with it. We do not become supporters of capitalism, but we accept that there is nothing that can be done about it. Disillusion is a falling into identification, an acceptance that what is, is; an active participation, then, in the separation of doing and done.

10 **The only way to break the apparently closed circle of power is by seeing that the transformation of power-to into power-over is a process which necessarily implies the existence of its opposite: fetishisation implies anti-fetishisation.**

Most discussions of alienation (fetishism, reification, discipline, identification and so on) treat it as though it were an accomplished fact. They treat the forms of capitalist social relations as though they were established at the dawn of capitalism and will continue until capitalism is replaced by another mode of social organisation. In other words, existence is separated from constitution: the constitution of capitalism is located in the historical past, its present existence is assumed to be stable. Such a view can only lead to a deep pessimism.

If, however, we see the separation of doing and done not as an accomplished fact but as a process, then the world begins to change. The very fact that we speak of alienation means that alienation cannot be complete. If separation, alienation (etc) is understood as a process, then this implies that its course is not pre-determined, that the transformation of power-to into power-over is always open, always at issue. A process implies a movement of becoming, implies that that which is in process (alienation) is and is not. Alienation, then, is a movement against its own negation, against anti-alienation. The existence of alienation implies the existence of anti-alienation. The existence of power-over implies the existence of anti-power-over, or, in other words, the movement of emancipation of power-to.

That which exists in the form of its negation, that which exists in the mode of being denied, really exists, in spite of its negation, as the negation of the process of denial. Capitalism is based on the denial of power-to, of humanity, of creativity, of dignity: but that does not mean that these cease to exist. As the Zapatistas have shown us, dignity exists in spite of its own negation. It does not stand on its own, but exists in the only form in which it can exist in this society, as struggle against its own negation. Power-to exists too: not as an island within a sea of power-over, but in the only form in which it can exist, as struggle against its own negation. Freedom too exists, not in the way that liberals present it, as something independent of social antagonisms, but in the only way it can exist in a society characterised by relations of domination, as struggle against that domination.

The real, material existence of that which exists in the form of its own negation, is the basis of hope.

11 **The possibility of changing society radically depends on the material force of that which exists in the mode of being denied.**

The material force of the negated can be seen in a number of ways. Firstly, it can be seen in the infinite number of struggles which do not aim at winning power-over others, but simply at asserting our own power-to, our own resistance against being dominated by others. These take many different forms, from open rebellion to struggles to gain or defend control over the labour process, or the processes of health or education, to the more fragmented, often silent, assertions of dignity (by children or women) within the home. The struggle for dignity, for that which is denied by existing society, can be seen too in many forms that are not overtly political, in literature, in music, in fairy tales. The struggle against inhumanity is ubiquitous, for it is implicit in our very existence as humans.

Secondly, the force of the negated can be seen in the dependence of power-over upon that which it negates. Those whose power-to lies in their capacity to tell others what to do always depend for their existence on the doing of those others. The whole history of domination can be seen as the struggle of the powerful to liberate themselves from their dependence on the powerless. The transition from feudalism to capitalism can be seen in this light, not just as the struggle of the serfs to free themselves from the lords, but as the struggle of the lords to free themselves from their serfs by converting their power into money and so into capital. The same search for freedom from the workers can be seen in the introduction of machinery, or in the massive conversion of productive capital into money capital, which plays such an important part in contemporary capitalism. In each case, the flight of the powerful from the doers is in vain. There is no way in which power-over can be anything other than the metamorphosis of power-to. There is no way in which the powerful can escape from their dependence upon the powerless.

This dependence manifests itself, thirdly, in the instability of the powerful, in the tendency of capital to crisis. Capital's flight from labour, through the replacement of labour by machines and by its conversion into money, is confronted by its ultimate dependence upon labour (that is, upon its capacity to convert human doing into abstract value-producing labour) in the form of falling rates of profit. What manifests itself in crisis is the force of that which capital denies, namely non-subordinate power-to-do.

12 Revolution is urgent but uncertain, a question and not an answer.

Orthodox-Marxist theories sought to win certainty over to the side of revolution, arguing that historical development led inevitably to the creation of a communist society. This is fundamentally misconceived, because there can be nothing certain about the creation of a self-determining society. Certainty can only be on the side of domination. Certainty is to be found in the homogenisation of time, in the freezing of doing into being. Self-determination is inherently uncertain. The death of the old certainties is to be welcomed as a liberation.

For the same reasons, revolution cannot be understood as an answer, but only as a question, as an exploration in the creation of dignity. Asking we walk.

22

Phil Hearse
Change the world without taking power?

2003

On John Holloway's book **Change the World Without Taking Power, The Meaning of Revolution Today,** Pluto Press 2002 (pbk). *This review was first published at http://www.marxsite.com*

Discussing the ideas in this book is useful, not because John Holloway has legions of devoted followers, but because many of the ideas he advances about fundamental social change are widespread in the global justice movement and anti-war movement internationally.

The idea of refusing to take power was popularised recently by Subcommandante Marcos, leader of the Zapatistas. Like much of what the Subcommandante says, this was very ambiguous, because in any case the EZLN, representing indigenous people in a small corner of Mexico, cannot possibly take power – at least on its own[1]. However, the basic idea of revolutionising social relations without conquering power has been around a long time.

Although Holloway has some critical things to say about Tronti and Antonio Negri, intellectual parents of the Italian autonomia currents, his main arguments come directly from them: don't confront the power of the bosses in the world of work, withdraw from it. Create autonomous spaces – autonomous from the bosses, autonomous from the capitalist state. Of course this means struggle, but not the elaborate apparatuses of political parties or taking state power.

Some of the things that Holloway says in the course of his argument are very widespread today's radical movements; they go the heart of revolutionary strategy, and explicitly Holloway's main polemical target is revolutionary marxism.

Reviewing a book like this means lengthy quotes so readers can judge the argument for themselves: but to anticipate, key Holloway arguments are:

1 Reformism and revolutionary marxism both have as their strategic objective capturing state or governmental power; but this is a trap, since the state is inevitably an authoritarian structure. (Bog standard anarchism, that one).

2 The state is not the locus of power; capitalist social relations are where power lies. Orthodox Marxists don't see that the state is firmly embedded in capitalist social relations and that merely capturing it changes little, since authoritarian social relations remain in place.

3 Capitalist social relations can only be changed by alternative social practices that are generated by the oppressed themselves, in the course of resistance and struggle.

4 The theoretical basis of this argument is the category of (commodity) fetishism and its reproduction. Social relations are not a structure or a 'thing', but a relationship which is daily reproduced in the process of 'fetishisation'. But this reproduction is not automatic and can be disrupted by alternative social practices of resistance.

5 The claim by Engels and others that Marxism is a 'science' automatically generates an authoritarian practice; the oppressed are divided into those who 'know' (the vanguard, the party) and those who have false consciousness (the masses). A manipulative and substitutionist practice automatically results from this idea. Even Lukacs and Gramsci couldn't break out of this false problematic.

6 There are no guarantees of a happy ending; all that is possible is negative critique and resistance, and we shall see the outcome.

The State: "assassin of hope"

"What can we do to put an end to all the misery and exploitation?...There is an answer ready at hand. Do it through the state. Join a political party, help it to win governmental power, change the country in that way. Or, if you are more impatient, more angry, more doubtful about what can be achieved through parliamentary means, join a revolutionary organisation, help conquer state power by violent or non-violent means, and then use the revolutionary state to change society.

"Change the world through the state: this is the paradigm that has dominated revolutionary thought for more than a century. The debate between Rosa Luxemburg and Eduard Bernstein a hundred years ago on 'reform or revolution' established the terms which were to dominate thinking about revolution for most of the 20th century...The intensity of the disagreements concealed a basic point of agreement: both approaches focus on the state as the vantage point from society can be changed..." [2]

But this has been a trap, because:

"If the state paradigm was the vehicle of hope for much of the century, it became more and more an assassin of hope as the century progressed....For over a hundred years the revolutionary enthusiasm of young people has been channeled into building the party or into learning to shoot guns; for over a hundred years the dreams of those who wanted a world fit for humanity have been bureaucratised and militarised, all for the winning of state power by a government that could then be accused of 'betraying' the movement that put it there....Rather than look to so many betrayals as an explanation, perhaps we need to look at the very notion that society can be changed through winning state power." [3]

What theoretical error lies behind this trap?

"[Revolutionary movements inspired by Marxism] have often had an instrumental view of the capitalist nature of the state. They have typically seen the state as being the instrument of the capitalist class. The notion of an 'instrument' implies the relation between the state and the capitalist class is an external one; like a hammer the state is wielded by the capitalist class in its own interests, while after the revolution it will be wielded by the working class in their interests. Such a view reproduces, unconsciously perhaps, the isolation or autonomisation of the state from its social environment, the critique of which is the starting point of revolutionary politics...this view fetishises the state: it abstracts from the web of power relations in which it is embedded... The mistake of the Marxist revolutionary movement has been, not to deny the capitalist nature of the state, but to misunderstand the degree of integration of the state into the networks of capitalist social relations." [4]

This leads to disastrous consequences for the movement:

"What was something initially negative (the rejection of capitalism) is converted into something positive (institution building, power-building). The induction into the conquest of power inevitably becomes an induction into power itself. The initiates lean the language, logic and calculations of power; they learn to wield the categories of a social science which has been entirely shaped by its obsession with power." [5]

This far from exhausts Holloway's line of reasoning about the state, and we go into subsidiary aspects below. However the critique of revolutionary marxism so far is very radical and raises many questions about the nature of capitalist society and how to change it. The following might be some initial points of reflection about Holloway's case.

First, Holloway knows but does not emphasise, that revolutionary marxists do not fight to capture the capitalist state, but to smash it. For him, the state is the state is the state, an unchanging category within which strictly limited sets of social relations can exist. His critique reads as if Lenin's *The State and Revolution* had never been written. But the marxist concept of revolution is not that the working class smashes the state and simply replaces it with a workers' state, through which social change can be effected. Our concept of the workers, socialist, 'state' is the democratic self-organisation of the masses, not the dictatorship of the party. Indeed we are not (or should not be) in favour of a monopoly by any one party.

Illogically, Holloway several times refers positively to the example of the Paris Commune. This of course was what inspired Lenin in *The State and Revolution*. Lenin argues for the 'Commune State'; that was the basis of his thinking on the subject. In this conception, *social relations are changed, or begin to be changed, directly and immediately through the process of socialist revolution*, not just through the change in the nature of the state, but in the changing social relations which accompany this process. In advanced capitalist countries at least, it is impossible to imagine the scale of social mobilisation required to overwhelm the capitalist state, without at the same time − or in very short order − the popular masses seizing democratic control of the factories, offices and companies. Our concept of revolution is not simply 'capturing' the state and wielding it in the interests of the masses − that is the (old) social democratic idea; our alternative is the masses smashing the state in a huge social uprising and democratising power, governing through their own institutions of power.

Holloway's argument about the state being 'embedded' in capitalist social relations is correct as far as it goes, but is unidirectional. The state is not just buried in the web of capitalist social relations, it is essential for the functioning of capitalism. It is where much of the essential and strategic decision making is centered. It is the crucial defence mechanism against social relations being fundamentally changed.

Holloway's argument is basically that if you have any kind of state, you have oppression and capitalism. It's easy to see the illogicality of this argument. Let us change, for the sake of argument, the revolutionary marxist traditional phraseology. Let's abandon the idea of a workers' state, and say we want the *direct administration of social affairs by the democratically organised masses*. Naturally, they will have to elect recallable officials, have meetings in enterprises, offices and schools and vote on what to do. They may need some kind of national assembly and elected officials of that assembly to carry out executive functions. If all that is rejected, it is difficult to imagine how the basic functioning of society could be decided and effected. Strangely (or perhaps wisely from his viewpoint) Holloway just doesn't discuss any element of post-revolutionary society, its decision-making or mechanisms of administration. Because if you do discuss that, you end up talking about something that sounds very like some kind of state.

This leads to a strange paradox in his argument, to which Holloway is blind. For the sake of argument, let's say that the Zapatista base communities are a good model of changed social relations and self-government. Let's say we want to 'Zapatistise' the whole of Mexico. But in Holloway's schema you can't – because you would build, in this process, a state – a 'Zapatista state'. So you evacuate national (and international) terrains of struggle, concentrate on the local and the particular. Which can only lead to the capitalist class saying 'thank you very much'.

The reproduction of capitalist social relations

Holloway invents his own phraseology to describe capitalist social relations. Capitalist power is 'power over' which confronts 'power to', and subjugates the 'social flow of doing'. This needn't bother us too much, because 'power over' turns out to be 'the power of the done', ie the power of accumulated capital against the creativity of living labour. 'Power to', sometimes described as 'anti-power', can confront 'power over'. "It is the movement of power-to, the struggle to emancipate human potential, that provides the perspective of breaking the circle of domination. It is only through the practice of emancipation, of power-to, that power-over can be overcome (my emphasis PH). Work, then, remains central to any discussion of revolution, but only if the starting point of that is not labour, not fetishised work, but rather work as doing, as the creativity or power-to that exists as, but also against-and-beyond labour." [6]

This can take place within the following perspective:

"In the process of struggle-against, relations are formed which are not the mirror image of the relations of power against which the struggle is directed: relations of comradeship, of solidarity, of love, relations which prefigure the sort of society we are struggling for....(The struggle against capitalism) and the struggle for emancipation cannot be separated, even when those in struggle are not conscious of the link. The most liberating struggles, however, are surely those in which the two are consciously linked, as in those struggles which are consciously prefigurative, in which the struggle aims, in its forms, not to reproduce the structures and practices of that which is struggles against, but rather to create the sort of social relations which are desired." [7]

In this context Holloway mentions for example factory occupations which are not just acts of resistance, but in which production is continued under workers control, for socially desirable ends. But Holloway contests what he sees as the narrowness of the left's view of what is 'political' and what is the exercise of 'anti-power':

"Anti-power is in the dignity of everyday existence. Anti-power is in the relations we form all the time, relations of love, friendship, comradeship, community, cooperation. Obviously such relations are traversed by power because of the nature of the society in which we live, yet the element of love, friendship, comradeship, lies in the constant struggle we wage against power, to establish those relations on the basis of mutual recognition, the mutual recognition of one another's dignity.....To think of opposition to capitalism only in terms of overt militancy is to see only the smoke rising from the volcano. Dignity (anti-power) exists wherever humans live. Oppression implies the opposite, the struggle to live as humans. In all that we live every day, illness, the educational system, sex, children, friendship, poverty, whatever, there is the struggle to do things with dignity, to do things right." [8]

A lot could be said about these ideas. Holloway is surely right in seeing a constant resentment against the effects of capitalism, a constant struggle against the effects of capitalist power in small as well as big things, and a constant struggle among large sections of the oppressed to create relations of mutual support with friends, family and workmates. But that's just one side of it. Lots of pettiness, meanness, jealousy, competition, violence, racism, sexism, criminality which targets other sections of the oppressed etc exists among the oppressed as well. The precise balance we can discuss. The issue, the strategic question, is *whether alternative (stable and permanent) social relations can be generated by alternative daily practices of resistance.* Holloway attempts to justify his view that they can by his adroit theoretical move on the question of fetishisation. According to him fetishised social relations are a process and not a structure:

"The understanding of fetishisation as a process is key to thinking about changing the world without taking power. If we abandon fetishisation-as-process, we abandon revolution as self-emancipation. The understanding of fetishism as hard fetishism can lead to understanding of revolution as changing the world on behalf of the oppressed, and this inevitably means a focus on taking power. Taking power is a political goal that makes sense of the idea of taking power 'on behalf of': a revolution which is not 'on behalf of' but self-moving has no need to even think of 'taking power'. [9]

At the root of this argument is a giant non-sequitur. The premise of fetishisation-as-process doesn't lead to the strategic conclusions that Holloway asserts. Let's look at the argument in more detail.

First, are fetishised social relations a structure or a process? Capitalist social relations have to be constantly reproduced and to that extent they are certainly a process. But they also pre-exist; they have been definitely constituted and are not subject to daily disruption and collapse (which is why Holloway's notion of the permanent crisis and instability of capitalism is wrong – see below). Every time workers turn up for work, the social relations of capitalism exploitation do not have to be re-made or re-invented; of course they are reproduced, if you want they are reiterated – but that is the normal process of capitalist reproduction. Looked at from the reverse angle, capitalist social relations are not daily challenged, threatened or put in question. That only *begins* to happen at times of acute political crisis, of revolutionary or pre-revolutionary upsurge. Because he lacks any notion of the political, Holloway must remain literally speechless in front of such events.

But it is these moments of crisis that the issue of 'power' is put on the table. What would Holloway have said, for example, to the revolutionary workers in Catalonia in 1936-7. Create alternative social relations, on a non-capitalist basis? But that is exactly what they did start to do, as anyone with a passing familiarity to those events will know. Firms were collectivised, land was seized by the peasants, the basis of an alternative, popular system of administration based on the committees and collectives could be seen in outline. Ditto in Chile 1971-3. Ditto in Portugal 1974-5; and many other examples could be quoted. But what happened? In each of those cases the revolutionary mass 'vanguard' was unable to seize or consolidate national political (state) power, and they were defeated, isolated, crushed – in Spain and Chile with terrifying and bloody consequences. By abandoning the terrain of the political and the strategic, Holloway's ideas leave the decisive arena of struggle to capitalist or pro-capitalist forces who will inevitably occupy it, preventing revolutionary change.

Now I'm going to parade some evidence strongly in favour of Holloway's position and against what has been said above. A recent article in the London *Observer* gave a fascinating insight into the struggles in the poor barrios of Caracas, focus of the Bolivarian 'revolution' in Hugo Chavez's Venezuela. Local people are taking over the running of their own lives in a gigantic scale. Water and electricity, schools, food aid for the poorest – every aspect of local administration is being taken over by the people themselves. One local activist is quoted as saying *"We don't want a government – we want to be the government"*. Surely this kind of activity is exactly what Holloway is talking about?

The statement by the local activist encapsulates an entirely positive and progressive attitude, a revolutionary attitude, to capitalism and the capitalist state. But then how can 'we', the people, the poor, the excluded, 'be the government'. That's the crux of the matter. Anyone who says to these activists "do exactly what you are doing, period" is doing them a big disservice. Their ability to begin to change social relations at a local level depends on the national political process, the whole 'Bolivarian' process and the existence of the Chavez government. If Chavez is brought down by local reaction and American imperialism, these local experiments in people's power will be crushed. That's the weakness of not integrating local process of power-changing with the national struggle for an alternative national state.

The article referred to above has interesting hints of conflict between the Bolivarian committees and some local activists, with the latter expressing resentment at local 'politicos' trying to intrude on their struggles. Such conflicts – which also occurred in Argentina – are a normal and inevitable part of revolutionary change. They are in reality a debate over perspectives. And it's natural that for some activists the whole huge project of changing the government and the state sometimes seems abstract and utopian, contrasted with the eminently practical tasks of solving people's needs here and now. Such attitudes are reinforced by the real manipulative and bureaucratic practices found in some organisations of the revolutionary and not-so-revolutionary left. But in the end they are wrong and self-defeating.

In accepting that social relations can be directly transformed simply by the social practices of the oppressed, Holloway abandons the terrain of strategy, and indeed of politics altogether. Marxists are bound to say to him that revolutionaries must, in one sense, be 'initiates' in power, learning the tricks and tactics of the very sordid business of politics. There are indeed negative consequences from this. It would be very nice indeed to proceed straight to alternative social relations without going through all this disgusting, murky business of building parties and fighting for power. As Ernest Mandel would have said, this is unfortunately impossible in 'this wicked world of ours'.

Holloway's pure naivety on this is revealed in a very interesting section on the struggles of 'anti-power:

"Look at the world around us, look beyond the newspapers, beyond the institutions of the labour movement and you can see a world of struggle: the autonomous municipalities in Chiapas, the students at the Universidad Nacional Autónoma de Mexico, the Liverpool dockers, the wave of international demonstrations against the power of money capital, the struggle of migrant workers...There is a whole world of struggle that does not aim at winning power, a whole world of struggle against power-over...There is a whole world of struggle that...develops forms of self-determination and develops an alternative conceptions of how the world should be." [10]

Well, true, sort of. But if we scratch the surface of the three particular struggles Holloway mentions, then we get a slightly different story. First, the Liverpool dockers. A struggle by a smallish group of workers, which was internationalised in an exemplary way, with solidarity actions from dockers and seafarers on several continents. Behind the scenes, however, several British Marxist organisations devoted considerable time and energy to building that struggle and creating the international links. That struggle would not have proceeded in the way it did without that intervention. Holloway doesn't know the facts perhaps, but I can give him the names and phone numbers of key revolutionary full-timers involved.

Second, the UNAM students one-year struggle against the imposition of student fees (1998-9). John Holloway should know more about that because much of his time is spent in Mexico. That struggle was led (I would say in some ways mis-led) by a coalition of rather ultra-left Marxist groups. For better or worse, they were able to rely on the support of up to five or six thousand of the most determined strikers, who could lead the others. It was not a struggle without political leadership; that leadership does indeed want to gain power, but given their ultra-left semi-Stalinist character, have no chance of succeeding – anyway, let's hope not.

Finally, what about the Holloway's key inspiration, the Zapatistas? The autonomous village assemblies are indeed exemplary, but from what exactly are they autonomous? Not political organisation and leadership, for absolute certainty. The Zapatista movement has three wings: the EZLN, the armed fighters; the base communities in the highland villages; and the Frente Zapatista, the FZLN, the nationwide support organisation. Leading all three politically is the Clandestine Indigenous Revolutionary Committee, precise membership unknown (ie it is clandestine), with a key figure being Subcommandante Marcos.

This is the leadership of a political organisation, which is in effect an ersatz political party, notwithstanding the denials of the Subcommandante and his followers. You can be absolutely sure that if the base communities are debating an important question, it will have first been discussed in the clandestine leadership based in the selva. Village democracy is not exactly spontaneous.

Equally, the FZLN do not do a single thing without it being personally authorised by the Subcommandante. The democracy of the FZLN is not exactly transparent. If it has not become a nationwide party, it is partly because Marcos did not want it to escape his control.

Marxism, science, consciousness

To anticipate a little, John Holloway's case against the idea that Marxism is some kind of science consists of the following key points.

1 Marxists after Engels have held the view that science in general and Marxism in particular seek objective knowledge of the real world. Revolutionary theory by contrast is critical and negative; objective knowledge is impossible.

2 Engels and subsequent Marxists made Marxism a teleology – ie history is a process with an inevitable outcome – socialism. This downplays and eliminates the role of struggle.

3 By seeing the party (or the proletarian vanguard) as possessing knowledge which the masses do not posses, orthodox Marxists set up an authoritarian and manipulative relationship between the party and the masses. The category of false consciousness must be rejected, we are all victims of fetishisation, Marxist militants included. Gramsci's notion of hegemony is thus wrong.

4 By posing an end-point or goal for the struggle (ie socialism or communism), orthodox Marxists inevitably attempt to 'channel' and direct the struggles of the masses towards their preconceived ends. The notion of revolutionary rupture is imposed on the struggle from 'the outside'.

To answer all these points in detail would take a long book, but the main answer which revolutionary marxists should give to this charge sheet is 'not guilty'. However, some of the individual points contain an element of truth, in particular in relation to the Marxism of the Second International, and the 'Marxism' of Stalinism internationally. But many of the views ascribed to revolutionary marxism by Holloway are just not held by most people in the movement who think about these things.

Is Marxism a science? Does science provide objective knowledge of the world? Is such knowledge possible? Before giving some provisional answer to those questions, it should be said that Holloway's own answer to them – a bowdlerisation of ideas from the Frankfurt School – cannot be accepted:

"The concept of fetishism implies a negative concept of science...The concept of fetishism implies therefore that there is a radical distinction between 'bourgeois' science and critical or revolutionary science. The former assumes the permanence of capitalist social relations and takes identity for granted, treating contradiction as a mark of logical inconsistency. Science in this view is an attempt to understand reality. In the latter case, science can only be negative, a critique of the untruth of existing reality. The aim is not to understand reality, but to understand (and, by understanding, to intensify) its contradictions as part of the struggle to change the world. The more all-pervasive we understand reification to be, the more absolutely negative science becomes. If everything is permeated by reification, then absolutely everything is a site of struggle between the imposition of the rupture of doing and the critical-practical struggle for recuperation of doing. No category is neutral."[11]

A first thing which is obvious about this passage is the idea that science which wants to understand the world can't tolerate contradiction, because this is a sign of logical inconsistency. Any Marxist will tell you that our view is that contradiction in reality (not just thought) is a fundamental epistemological proposition of any real science.

In general Holloway's arguments pose completely false alternatives. One reading of it could postulate an absolute break between 'revolutionary' science and 'bourgeois' science; the worst consequences of that idea were the bizarre products of the Soviet academy. If followed logically, Holloway's idea of science would lead to a rejection of Nils Bohr or Alert Einstein on the grounds that their insights into wave and particle theory, or relativity, were not part of the struggle to change the world.

Most Marxists would argue that science has to be critical and 'dialectical' to produce knowledge, attempting to understand the contradictions in reality, social as well as physical. This 'dialectical' approach has been massively aided by the advent of chaos theory, which has struck a tremendous blow against the false dichotomies which bourgeois philosophy opened up between determinism and indeterminism. Chaos theory has shown that events can be determined, ie have causes which can be established, but also have indeterminate, unpredictable outcomes. Far from being a rejection of dialectical thought, this insight is a confirmation of it, or rather a deepening of it. (An extended discussion of these themes can be found in Daniel Bensaïd's book *Marx for Our Times*). But it is true that the insights of chaos theory are incompatible with the view of scientific predictability advanced by Engels in his famous 'parallelogram of forces'.

A number of consequences for our ideas about science follow. To say that science can produce knowledge of the real world is not the same thing as saying that the outcomes of all events can be predicted, not because we lack sufficient knowledge about causes, but by definition. Chaos theory has shown the limits of prediction, but they are not absolute. The range of possible outcomes of many physical and social processes can be known and predicted in advance. If this was not so, all science would be useless. We could never build a bridge, invent a new medicine or walk down the street.

John Holloway establishes a false polarity between positive and negative science, between knowledge and critique. It is possible to produce real knowledge of the world without that being part of the revolutionary struggle. It is also possible to produce real knowledge of social processes, without that leading to the view that social reality is governed by impermeable 'objective laws' with an inevitable outcome.

Thus, few Marxists today would argue that socialism is 'inevitable', that history has a preconceived end or outcome. Socialism is an objective, a goal we fight for, but it is the product of theoretical reflection. But not just that. That theoretical reflection is itself a reflection of contradictions in reality, ie the class struggle in capitalist society. To misquote Marx, theory tends towards reality and (hopefully) reality towards theory.

John Holloway claims Marxists think they possess objective knowledge that the masses do not:

"The notion of Marxism as science implies a distinction between those who know and those who do not know, a distinction between those who have true consciousness and those who have false consciousness...Political debate become focused on the question of 'correctness' and the 'correct line'. But how do we know (and how do they know) that the knowledge of those who know is correct? How can the knowers (party, intellectuals, or whatever) be said to transcend the conditions of their social time and place in such a way to have gained a privileged knowledge of historical movement. Perhaps even more important politically: if a distinction is made between those who know and those who do not, and if understanding or knowledge is seen as important in guiding the political struggle, then what is the organisational relation between the knowers and the others (the masses)? Are those in the know to lead and educate the masses (as in the concept of the vanguard party) or is a communist revolution necessarily the work of the masses themselves (as 'left communists' such as Pennekoek maintained)?

"...The notion of objective laws opens up a separation between structure and struggle. Whereas the notion of fetishism suggests that everything is struggle, that nothing exists separately from the antagonisms of social relations, the notion of 'objective laws' suggests a duality between *an objective structural movement independent of people's will, on the one hand, and the subjective struggles for a better world on the other.*"[12]

When Marxists say that a certain view, or suggested course of action, is 'correct' they do not thereby ascribe the status of absolute, objective knowledge to this category – or at least they shouldn't. All knowledge is provisional and subject to falsification. When discussing a course of action, 'correct' usually is a short-hand for 'the most appropriate in the situation'. On the other hand, when Marxists say things like 'the invasion of Iraq is an example of imperialism' they are indeed suggesting the existence of a category in social reality which is knowable and revealed by theoretical abstraction. Holloway must agree that such a process is possible, otherwise he wouldn't have written his book.

Marxists do not claim they have 'true consciousness' (whatever that might be) against the false consciousness of the masses. But they do claim that critical social theory is possible, and that this can develop concepts which help us to understand the development of capitalism and the struggle against it. Holloway's suggestion that this is impossible, because Marxists are themselves products of particular times and social situations, is plainly ridiculous. Of course they are, and Marxism is the product of particular times and circumstances. Its concepts are provisional (not absolute knowledge) which provide a framework for understanding and acting on the world. This understanding is not absolute or 'objective', it is partial and fragmentary. Its criterion has to be whether it is useful for understanding the world and acting upon it. Its falsification has to be in practice and struggle. If we don't have this attitude to revolutionary theory, then we abandon not just the terrain of strategy and politics, but theory as well.

Holloway's notion that we are all products of fetishisation and reification should not necessarily lead him to reject the notion of false consciousness; he could equally well say we all have false consciousness. There is a kernel of truth to that. It's just that some people have a consciousness which is more false than others. That may sound like a joke, but if Holloway rejects it we really do get into ridiculous territory. Can John Holloway really say that the views of someone who is a racist and nationalist are as equally valid as those who are revolutionary internationalists? Marxist theory may be partial and conditional, but surely it approximates to an understanding of the world which is critical or the existing social order, and provides insights into its contradictions and the possibilities for changing it.

There are big dangers in Holloway's view. By effectively rejecting the idea of false consciousness, he rejects the notion of ideology as something separate from (but linked to) reification and fetishism. Underestimating ideology leads to a lack of understanding of the ideological apparatuses of modern capitalism, which are massively powerful in generating and reiterating fetishised, pro-capitalist views. A possible consequence of this, logically, is a lack of understanding of the centrality of ideological struggle, of the necessity for a ceaseless fight – in propaganda and agitation as well as 'theory' – against the 'false' ideas pumped out by the pro-capitalist media (and academy) on a daily basis. This counter-struggle does not emerge spontaneously on any effective national basis. It has to be organised. This was something that Lenin was trying to say in a much-misrepresented text he wrote in 1902. But that's another story.

Strategic conclusions: a world without left parties?

John Holloway doesn't have any strategic conclusions, and unapologetically. There is, he says, "no guarantee of a happy outcome". Here, unfortunately, we can only agree. But unlike recent detractors of revolutionary parties, he doesn't put up alternative organisations – social movements, NGOs – as competitors for the crown of the 'modern prince'. He doesn't deny the need for co-ordinations for particular purposes and struggles, or the need for political militants. However, he is not interested in new or alternative organisations. We should look at the movement not as organisation, but – inspired by the cycle of anti-capitalist demonstrations – as "a series of events". And that's it, full stop.

Happily Holloway's ideas, some of which are widespread, will not convince everybody. If by some unforeseen accident they did, the consequences would be catastrophic. Disband the left organisations and parties and disband the trade unions. Forget elections and the fight over government. All that remains is the struggle of 'power-to' against 'power over'.

Not only will these ideas not become hegemonic on the left, it is structurally impossible for them to do so, as a moment's thought will reveal. Imagine, in a party-less world, five or six friends in different parts of any country, involved in anti-war coalitions, get together and discuss politics. They find they agree on many things – not just war, but racism, poverty and capitalist power. They decide to hold regular meetings and invite others.

Next, they produce a small newsletter to sell to comrades in the anti-war coalitions. In six months they discover a hundred people are coming to their meetings, and decide to hold a conference. In effect, they have formed a political party. And – obviously – if nobody else on the leftforms an alternative, they'll have hundreds of members in a year. Revolutionary parties cannot be done away with, not until the work they have to do is done away with as well. The sooner the better.

Notes

1 John Holloway, *Change the World Without Taking Power, The Meaning of Revolution Today*, Pluto Press 2002, p. 11.

2 Op. cit., p.12.

3 Op. cit., p.13.

4 Op. cit., p.15.

5 Op. cit., p.153.

6 Op. cit., p.159.

7 Op. cit., p.156.

8 Op. cit., p.108.

9 Op. cit., p.156.

10 Op. cit., p.118.

11 A discussion on these issues will be found in Daniel Bensaïd's *Marx for Our Times* (Verso 2002)).

12 op. cit., p.122.

38

John Holloway
Power and the State

16 October 2004

This text is John Holloway's speech in the debate on 'Strategies for Social Transformation', at the European Social Forum, London, October 16, 2004. The other speakers were Fausto Bertinotti, Hilary Wainwright and Phil Hearse.

1 I assume that we are here because we agree on two basic points. Firstly, capitalism is a disaster for humanity and we urgently need a radical social change, a revolution. Secondly, we do not know how such a change can take place. We have ideas, but no certainties. That is why it is important to discuss, respecting our differences and understanding that we are all part of the same movement.

2 In this discussion, we start from where we are, from a confused movement, a cacophony of rebellions, loosely united in this Social Forum. The question is how we should continue. Should we organise as a party? Should we focus our struggles on the state and in winning influence within the state or conquering state power? Or should we turn our back on the state in so far as we can and get on with constructing an alternative? I want to argue that we should turn our back on the state in so far as possible.

3 This is a question of how we organise and where we think we are going. The state is a form of organisation, a way of doing things. The state is an organisation separate from the rest of society. The people who work in the state (the politicians and the functionaries or civil servants) work on behalf of society, for the benefit of society, as they see it. Some are better than others (I have no doubt that Bertinotti is better than Berlusconi), but all work on our behalf, in our name. In other words, they exclude us.

The state, as an organisational form, is a way of excluding us, of negating the possibility of self-determination. Once we are excluded, we have no real control over what they do. Representative democracy reinforces and legitimates our exclusion, it does not give us control over what the state does. Many of the worst atrocities are justified in the name of democracy.

If we focus our struggles on the state, we have to understand that the state pulls us in a certain direction. Above all, it seeks to impose upon us a separation of our struggles from society, to convert our struggle into a struggle on behalf of, in the name of. It separates leaders from the masses, the representatives from the represented, it draws us into a different way of talking, a different way of thinking. It pulls us into a process of reconciliation with reality, and that reality is the reality of capitalism, a form of social organisation that is based on exploitation and injustice, on killing and destruction. There is one key concept in the history of the state-centred left, and that concept is betrayal. Time and time again, the leaders have betrayed the movement, and not necessarily because they are bad people, but just because the state as a form of organisation separates the leaders from the movement and draws them into a process of reconciliation with capital. Betrayal is already given in the state as an organisational form.

Can we resist this? Yes, of course we can, and it is something that happens all the time. We can refuse to let the state identify leaders or permanent representatives of the movement, we can refuse to let delegates negotiate in secret with the representatives of the state. But this means understanding that our forms of organisation are very different from those of the state, that there is no symmetry between them. The state is an organisation on behalf of, what we want is the organisation of self-determination, a form of organisation that allows us to articulate what we want, what we decide, what we consider necessary or desirable – a council or communal organisation, a commun-ism. There are no models for how we should organise our drive towards self-determination. It is always a matter of invention and experimentation. What is clear is that the state as a form of organisation pushes in the opposite direction, against self-determination. The two forms of organisation are incompatible.

When I say "state", I include parties or any organisation that has the state as its main focus. The party, as a form of organisation, reproduces the state form: it excludes, it creates distinctions between leaders and masses, representatives and represented; in order to win state power, it adopts the agenda and the temporalities of the state. In other words, it goes against the drive towards social self-determination which I think is the core of our struggle. Note that I am saying to Fausto and to Daniel and to Hilary "I don't think the party is the right way to organise". I am not saying "I don't like you" or "I will not cooperate with you", nor am I saying that struggles that take another route (such as the case of Venezuela) are therefore to be condemned. I am simply saying that in thinking of the way forward, party organisation or focussing on state power is the wrong way to go, because it implies a form of organisation that excludes and imposes hierarchies, that weakens and bureaucratises the anarchic effervescence of the drive towards self-determination that is the core of the current movement against neo-liberal capitalism.

4. What does it mean to turn our back on the state? In some cases, it means ignoring the state completely, not making any demands on the state, just getting on with the construction of our own alternatives. The most obvious example of that at the moment would be the Zapatistas' shift in direction last year, their creation of the Juntas de Buen Gobierno, the creation of their own regional administration in a way that seeks to avoid the separation of administration and society typical of the state.

In other cases, it is difficult to turn our back on the state completely, because we need its resources in order to live – as teachers, as students, as unemployed, whatever. It is very difficult for most of us to avoid all contact with the state. In that case, what is important is to understand that the state is a form of organisation that pulls us in certain directions, that pulls us towards a reconciliation with capitalism, and to think how we can shape our contact with the state, how we can move against-and-beyond the state as a form of doing things, refusing to accept the creation of hierarchies, the fragmentation of our struggles that contact with the state implies, refusing to accept the language and the logic and perhaps above all the temporality of the state, the times and rhythms that the state tries to impose on us. How do we engage with the state without slotting in to its logic, without reproducing its logic inside our own movement? This is always a difficult issue in practice, in which it is very easy to get drawn into the logic of achieving particular concrete aims and forget the impact on the dynamic of the movement as a whole. I do not think it is a question of reclaiming the state, although I have a lot of respect for many of the struggles that are covered in Hilary's book, but I think the idea of reclaiming the state is wrong: the state is an alien form of organisation – it is not, and cannot be, ours.

5. In all this the question of time and how we think about time is crucial. On the one hand the state imposes its temporality on us all the time, with its rhythm of elections and its changes of regime which change little or nothing: "Wait till the next election and then you can change things; if you want to do something now, then prepare for the next election, build the party". On the other hand, the Leninist revolutionary tradition also tells us to wait: "Wait for the next revolutionary occasion or the next downturn of the long wave, wait until we take power and then we shall change society; in the meantime, build the party".

But we know that we cannot wait. Capitalism is destroying the world and destroying us at such a rate that we cannot wait. We cannot wait for the election and we cannot wait for the revolution, we cannot wait until we win state power in one way or another, we have to try and break the destructive dynamic now. We have to refuse. Capitalism does not exist because the evil ones, the Bushes and Blairs and Berlusconis, create it. Capitalism does not exist because it was created a hundred or two hundred years ago. Capitalism exists today only because we created it today. If we do not create capitalism tomorrow, then it will not exist tomorrow. Capitalism exists because we make it, and we have to stop making it, to refuse. This means breaking time, breaking continuity, understanding that something does not exist today just because it existed yesterday: it exists only if we make it.

In thinking about alternatives to the state, I think refusal has to be the pivot, the key. But it is not enough. To maintain our refusal to make capitalism, we have to have an alternative way of surviving. The refusal has to be accompanied by the creation of a different world, the creation of a new commons, the creation of a different way of doing things. Behind the absolute here-and-now of refusal there has to be another temporality, a patient construction of a different world. There is no model for this. The only model is the multiplicity of experiences and inventions of the movement of resistance against capitalism. This multiplicity, this cacophony of struggles and experiences should be respected, not channelled into a party, not focussed on the winning of state power. The problem is not to take power, but to construct our own power, our own power to do things differently, our own power to create a different world.

Daniel Bensaïd
On a recent book by John Holloway

2005

Can we speak of a libertarian current, as if this continuous thread were unrolling throughout contemporary history, as if it were possible to tie a sufficient number of affinities to it to make what holds it together win out over what divides it? Such a current, if in fact it exists, is indeed characterised by a considerable theoretical eclecticism, and crosscut by strategic orientations that not only diverge but also often contradict each other. We can nonetheless maintain the hypothesis that there is a libertarian 'tone' or 'sensibility' that is broader than anarchism as a specifically defined political position. It is thus possible to speak of a libertarian communism (exemplified notably by Daniel Guérin), a libertarian messianism (Walter Benjamin), a libertarian Marxism (Michael Löwy and Miguel Abensour), and even a 'libertarian Leninism' whose especial source is *State and Revolution*.

This 'family resemblance' (often torn apart and stitched back together) is not enough to found a coherent genealogy. We can instead refer to 'libertarian moments' registered in very different situations and drawing their inspiration from quite distinct theoretical sources. We can distinguish three key moments in rough outline:

1 A constituent (or classic) moment exemplified by the trio Stirner/ Proudhon/Bakunin. *The Ego and Its Own* (Stirner) and *The Philosophy of Poverty* (Proudhon) were published in the mid-1840s. During those same years Bakunin's thought was shaped over the course of a long and winding journey that took him from Berlin to Brussels by way of Paris. This was the watershed moment in which the period of post-revolutionary reaction drew to a close and the uprisings of 1848 were brewing. The modern state was taking shape. A new consciousness of individuality was discovering the chains of modernity in the pain of romanticism. An unprecedented social movement was stirring up the depths of a people that was being fractured and divided by the eruption of class struggle. In this transition, between 'already-no-longer' and 'not-yet', different forms of libertarian thought were flirting with blooming utopias and romantic ambivalences. A

dual movement was being sketched out of breaking with and being pulled towards the liberal tradition. Daniel Cohn-Bendit's identification with a 'liberal-libertarian' orientation follows in the footsteps of this formative ambiguity.

2 An anti-institutional or anti-bureaucratic moment, at the turn of the 19th and 20th centuries. The experience of parliamentarianism and mass trade unionism was revealing at that time 'the professional dangers of power' and the bureaucratisation threatening the labour movement. The diagnosis can be found in Rosa Luxemburg's work as well as in Robert Michels' classic book on *Political Parties* (1910)[1]; in the revolutionary syndicalism of Georges Sorel and Fernand Pelloutier; and equally in the critical fulgurations of Gustav Landauer. We also find traces of it in Péguy's *Cahiers de la Quinzaine*[2] or in Labriola's *Italian Marxism*.

3 A third, post-Stalinist moment responds to the great disillusionment of the tragic century of extremes. A neo-libertarian current, more diffuse but more influential than the direct heirs of classical anarchism, is confusedly emerging. It constitutes a state of mind, a 'mood', rather than a well-defined orientation. It is engaging with the aspirations (and weaknesses) of the renascent social movements. The themes of authors like Toni Negri and John Holloway[3] are thus much more inspired by Foucault and Deleuze than by historic 19th-century sources, of which classic anarchism itself scarcely exercises its right to make a critical inventory.[4]

Amidst these 'moments' we can find ferrymen (like Walter Benjamin, Ernst Bloch and Karl Korsch) who initiate the transition and critical transmission of the revolutionary heritage, 'rubbing against the grain' of the Stalinist glaciation.

The contemporary resurgence and metamorphoses of libertarian currents are easily explained:

– by the depth of the defeats and disappointments experienced since the 1930s, and by the heightened consciousness of the dangers that threaten a politics of emancipation from within;

– by the deepening of the process of individualisation and the emergence of an 'individualism without individuality', anticipated in the controversy between Stirner and Marx; and

– by the steadily fiercer forms of resistance to the disciplinary contrivances and procedures of bio-political control on the part of those who are being subjected to a subjectivity mutilated by market reification.

In this context, in spite of the profound disagreements that we will expound in this article, we are glad to grant Negri and Holloway's contributions the merit of relaunching a much-needed strategic debate in the movements of resistance to imperial globalisation, after a sinister quarter-century in which this kind of debate had withered away, while those who refused to surrender to the (un)reason of the triumphant market swung back and forth between a rhetoric of resistance without any horizon of expectation and the fetishist expectation of some miraculous event. We have taken up elsewhere the critique of Negri and his evolution.[5] Here we will begin a discussion with John Holloway, whose recent book bears a title that is a programme in itself and has already provoked lively debates in both the English-speaking world and Latin America.

Statism as original sin

In the beginning was the scream. John Holloway's approach starts from imperative of unconditional resistance: we scream! It is a cry not only of rage, but also of hope. We let out a scream, a scream against, a negative scream, the Zapatistas' scream in Chiapas – '*Ya Basta! Enough of this!*' – a scream of refusal to submit, of dissent. 'The aim of this book', Holloway announces from the start, 'is to strengthen negativity, to take the side of the fly in the web, to make the scream more strident[6]. What has brought the Zapatistas (whose experience haunts Holloway's disquisition throughout) together with others 'is not a positive common class composition but rather the community of their negative struggle against capitalism'[7]. Holloway is thus describing a struggle whose aim is to negate the inhumanity that has been imposed on us, in order to recapture a subjectivity that is immanent in negativity itself. We have no need of a promise of a happy end to justify our rejection of the world as it is. Like Foucault, Holloway wants stay connected with the million, multiple forms of resistance, which are irreducible to the binary relation between capital and labour.

Yet this way of taking sides by crying out is not enough. It is also necessary to be able to give an account of the great disillusionment of the last century. Why did all those cries, those millions of cries, repeated millions of times over, not only leave capital's despotic order standing but even leave it more arrogant than ever? Holloway thinks he has the answer. The worm was in the apple; that is, the (theoretical) vice was originally nestled inside the emancipatory virtue: statism was gnawing away at most variants of the workers' movement from the beginning. Changing the world by means of the state thus constituted in his eyes the dominant paradigm of revolutionary thought, which was subjected from the 19th century on to an instrumental, functional vision of the state. The illusion that society could be changed by means of the state flowed (Holloway says) from a certain idea of state sovereignty. But we have ended up learning that 'we cannot change the world through the state', which only constitutes 'a node in a web of power relations'[8]. This state must not be confused in fact with power. All it does is define the division between citizens and non-citizens (the foreigner, the excluded, Gabriel Tarde's man 'rejected by the world' or Arendt's pariah). The state is thus very precisely what the word suggests: 'a bulwark against change, against the flow of doing', or in other words 'the embodiment of identity'[9]. It is not a thing that can be laid hold of in order to turn it against those who have controlled it until now, but rather a social form, or, more accurately, a process of formation of social relations: 'a process of statification of social conflict'[10]. Claiming to struggle by means of the state thus leads inevitably to defeating oneself. Stalin's 'statist strategies' thus do not for Holloway constitute in any sense a betrayal of Bolshevism's revolutionary spirit, but its complete fulfilment: 'the logical outcome of a state-centred concept of social change'[11]. The Zapatista challenge by contrast consists of saving the revolution from the collapse of the statist illusion and at the same time from the collapse of the illusion of power.

Before we go any further in reading Holloway's book, it is already apparent:

That he has reduced the luxuriant history of the workers' movement, its experiences and controversies to a single line of march of statism through the ages, as if very different theoretical and strategic conceptions had not been constantly battling with each other. He thus presents an imaginary Zapatismo as something absolutely innovative, haughtily ignoring the fact that the actually existing Zapatista discourse bears within it, albeit without knowing it, a number of older themes.

By his account the dominant paradigm of revolutionary thought consists of a functionalist statism. We could accept that – only by swallowing the very dubious assumption that the majoritarian ideology of social democracy (symbolised by Noskes and other Eberts) and the bureaucratic Stalinist orthodoxy can both be subsumed under the elastic heading of 'revolutionary thought'. This is taking very little account of an abundant critical literature on the question of the state, which ranges from Lenin and Gramsci to contemporary polemics[12] by way of contributions that are impossible to ignore (whether one agrees with them or not) like those of Poulantzas and Altvater.

Finally, reducing the whole history of the revolutionary movement to the genealogy of a 'theoretical deviation' makes it possible to hover over real history with a flap of angelic wings, but at the risk of endorsing the reactionary thesis (from François Furet to Gérard Courtois) of an unbroken continuity from the October Revolution to the Stalinist counter-revolution – its 'logical outcome'! – incidentally without subjecting Stalinism to any serious analysis. David Rousset, Pierre Naville, Moshe Lewin, Mikaïl Guefter (not to speak of Trotsky or Hannah Arendt, or even of Lefort or Castoriadis), are far more serious on this point.

The vicious circle of fetishism, or how to get out of it?

The other source of the revolutionary movement's strategic divagations relates in Holloway's account to the abandonment (or forgetting) of the critique of fetishism that Marx introduced in the first volume of *Capital*. On this subject Holloway provides a useful, though sometimes quite sketchy, reminder. Capital is nothing other than past activity (dead labour) congealed in the form of property. Thinking in terms of property comes down however to thinking of property as a thing, in the terms of fetishism itself, which means in fact accepting the terms of domination. The problem does not derive from the fact that the capitalists own the means of production: 'Our struggle', Holloway insists, 'is not the struggle to make ours the property of the means of production, but to dissolve both property and means of production: to recover or, better, create the conscious and confident sociality of the flow of doing.'[13]

But how can the vicious circle of fetishism be broken? The concept, says Holloway, refers to the unbearable horror constituted by the self-negation of the act. He thinks that Capital is devoted above all to developing the critique of this self-negation. The concept of fetishism contains in concentrated form the critique of bourgeois society (its 'enchanted ... world'[14] and of bourgeois theory (political economy), and at the same time lays bare the reasons for their relative stability: the infernal whirligig that turns objects (money, machines, commodities) into subjects and subjects into objects. This fetishism worms its way into all the pores of society to the point that the more urgent and necessary revolutionary change appears, the more impossible it seems to become. Holloway sums this up in a deliberately disquieting turn of phrase: 'the urgent impossibility of revolution'[15].

This presentation of fetishism draws on several different sources: Lukács' account of reification, Horkheimer's account of instrumental rationality, Adorno's account of the circle of identity, and Marcuse's account of one-dimensional man. The concept of fetishism expresses for Holloway the power of capital exploding in our deepest selves like a missile shooting out a thousand coloured rockets. This is why the problem of revolution is not the problem of 'them' – the enemy, the adversary with a thousand faces – but first of all our problem, the problem that 'we', this 'we' fragmented by fetishism, constitute for ourselves.

The fetish, this 'real illusion', in fact enmeshes us in its toils and subjugates us. It makes the status of critique itself problematic: if social relationships are fetishised, how can we criticise them? And who, what superior and privileged beings, are the critics? In short, is critique itself still possible?

These are the questions, according to Holloway, that the notion of a vanguard, of an 'imputed' class consciousness (imputed by whom?), or the expectation of a redemptive event (the revolutionary crisis), claimed to answer. These solutions lead ineluctably to the problematic of a healthy subject or a champion of justice fighting against a sick society: a virtuous knight who could be incarnated in a 'working-class hero' or vanguard party.

This is a 'hard' conception of fetishism, which therefore leads to an insoluble double dilemma:

Is revolution conceivable? Is criticism still possible? How can we escape from this 'fetishisation of fetishism'? Who are we then to wield the corrosive power of critique? 'We are not God. We are not ... transcendent'![16] And how can we avoid the dead end of a subaltern critique that remains under the ascendancy of the fetish that it is claiming to overthrow, inasmuch as negation implies subordination to what it negates?

Holloway puts forward several solutions:

The reformist response, which concludes that the world cannot be radically transformed; we must content ourselves with rearranging it and fixing it around the edges. Today postmodernist rhetoric accompanies this form of resignation with its lesser chamber music.

The traditional revolutionary response, which ignores the subtleties and marvels of fetishism and clings to the good old binary antagonism between capital and labour, so as to content itself with a change of ownership at the summit of the state: the bourgeois state simply becomes proletarian.

A third way, which would consist by contrast of looking for hope in the very nature of capitalism and in its 'ubiquitous (or pluriform) power', to which a 'ubiquitous (or pluriform) resistance' is an appropriate response.[17]

Holloway believes that he can escape in this way from the system's circularity and deadly trap, by adopting a soft version of fetishism, understood not as a state of affairs but as a dynamic and contradictory process of fetishisation. He thinks this process is in fact pregnant with its contrary: the 'anti-fetishisation' of forms of resistance immanent to fetishism itself. We are not mere objectified victims of capital, but actual or potential antagonistic subjects: 'Our existence-against-capital' is thus 'the inevitable constant negation of our existence-in-capital'.[18]

Capitalism should be understood above all as separation from the subject and from the object, and modernity as the unhappy consciousness of this divorce. Within the problematic of fetishism the subject of capitalism is not the capitalist himself but the value that is valorised and becomes autonomous. Capitalists are nothing more than loyal agents of capital and of its impersonal despotism. But then for a functionalist Marxism capitalism appears as a closed, internally consistent system without any possible exit, at least until the arrival of the deus ex machina [o], the great miraculous moment of revolutionary upheaval. For Holloway by contrast the weakness of capitalism consists in the fact that capital 'is dependent on labour in a way in which labour is not dependent upon capital': the 'insubordination of labour is thus the axis on which the constitution of capital as capital turns'. In the relationship of reciprocal but asymmetrical dependency between capital and labour, labour is thus capable of freeing itself from its opposite while capital is not.[19]

Holloway thus draws his inspiration from the autonomist theses previously put forward by Mario Tronti, which reversed the terms of the dilemma by presenting capital's role as purely reactive to the creative initiative of labour. In this perspective labour, as the active element of capital, always determines capitalist development by means of class struggle. Tronti presented his approach as 'a Copernican revolution within Marxism'.[20] While beguiled by this idea, Holloway still has reservations about a theory of autonomy that tends to renounce the work of negation (and in Negri's case to renounce any dialectic in favour of ontology) and to treat the industrial working class as a positive, mythical subject (just as Negri treats the multitude in his last book). A radical inversion should not content itself with transferring capital's subjectivity to labour, Holloway says, but should rather understand subjectivity as a negation, not as a positive affirmation.

To conclude (provisionally) on this point, we should acknowledge the service John Holloway has done in putting the question of fetishism and reification back in the heart of the strategic enigma. We need nonetheless to note the limited novelty of his argument. While the 'orthodox Marxism' of the Stalinist period (including Althusser) had in fact discarded the critique of fetishism, its red thread had nevertheless never been broken: starting from Lukács, we can follow it through the works of the authors who belonged to what Ernst Bloch called 'the warm current of Marxism': Roman Rosdolsky, Jakubowski, Ernest Mandel, Henri Lefèbvre (in his Critique of Everyday Life), Lucien Goldmann, Jean-Marie Vincent (whose Fétichisme et Société dates back to 1973!)[21], and more recently Stavros Tombazos and Alain Bihr.[22]

Emphasising the close connection between the processes of fetishisation and anti-fetishisation, Holloway, after many detours, brings us once more to the contradiction of the social relationship that manifests itself in class struggle. Like Chairman Mao, he makes clear nonetheless that since the terms of the contradiction are not symmetrical, the pole of labour forms its dynamic, determinant element. It's a bit like the boy who wrapped his arm around his head in order to grab his nose. We may note however that Holloway's stress on the process of 'defetishisation' at work within fetishisation enables him to relativise ('defetishise'?) the question of property, which he declares without any further ado to be soluble in 'the flow of doing'.[23]

Questioning the status of his own critique, Holloway fails to escape from the paradox of the sceptic who doubts everything except his own doubt. The legitimacy of his own critique thus continues to hang on the question 'in whose name' and 'from which (partisan?) standpoint' he proclaims this dogmatic doubt (ironically underscored in the book by Holloway's refusal to bring it to a full stop). In short, 'Who are we, we who criticise?':[24] privileged, marginal people, decentred intellectuals, deserters from the system? Implicitly an intellectual elite, a kind of vanguard, Holloway admits. For once the choice has been made to dispense with or relativise class struggle, the role of the free-floating intellectual paradoxically emerges reinforced. We then quickly fall back once more into the – Kautskyist rather than Leninist – idea of science being brought by the intelligentsia 'into the proletarian class struggle from without' (by intellectuals in possession of scientific knowledge), rather than Lenin's idea of 'class political consciousness' (not science!) brought 'from outside the economic struggle' (not from outside the class struggle) by a party (not by a scientific intelligentsia).[25]

Decidedly, taking fetishism seriously does not make it easier to dispose of the old question of the vanguard, whatever word you use for it. After all, isn't Zapatismo still a kind of vanguard (and Holloway its prophet)?

'The urgent impossibility of revolution'

Holloway proposes to return to the concept of revolution 'as a question, not as an answer'[26] What's at stake in revolutionary change is no longer 'taking power' for Holloway but the very existence of power: 'The problem of the traditional concept of revolution is perhaps not that it aimed too high, but that it aimed too low'.[27] In fact, 'The only way in which revolution can now be imagined is not as the conquest of power but as the dissolution of power.' This and nothing else is what the Zapatistas, frequently cited as a reference point, mean when they declare that they want to create a world of humanity and dignity, 'but without taking power'. Holloway admits that this approach may not seem very realistic. While the experiences that inspire him have not aimed at taking power, neither have they – so far – succeeded in changing the world. Holloway simply (dogmatically?) asserts that there is no other way.

This certainty, however peremptory it may be, hardly brings us much further. How to change the world without taking power? The book's author confides in us.

At the end of the book, as at the beginning, we do not know. The Leninists know, or used to know. We do not. Revolutionary change is more desperately urgent than ever, but we do not know any more what revolution means.... (O)ur not-knowing is ... the not-knowing of those who understand that not-knowing is part of the revolutionary process. We have lost all certainty, but the openness of uncertainty is central to revolution. 'Asking we walk', say the Zapatistas. We ask not only because we do not know the way ...but also because asking the way is part of the revolutionary process itself.[28]

So here we are at the heart of the debate. On the threshold of the new millennium, we no longer know what future revolutions will be like. But we know that capitalism will not be eternal, and that we urgently need to cast it off before it crushes us. This is the first meaning of the idea of revolution: it expresses the recurrent aspiration of the oppressed to their liberation. We also know – after the political revolutions that gave birth to the modern nation-state, and after the trials of 1848, the Commune and the defeated revolutions of the 20th century – that the revolution will be social or it will not be. This is the second meaning that the word revolution has taken on, since the *Communist Manifesto*. But on the other hand, after a cycle of mostly painful experiments, we have difficulty imagining the strategic form of revolutions to come. It is this third meaning of the word that escapes our grasp. This is not terribly new: nobody had planned the Paris Commune, soviet power or the Catalan Council of Militias. These forms of revolutionary power, 'found at last', were born of the struggle itself and from the subterranean memory of previous experiences.

Have so many beliefs and certainties vanished in mid-career since the Russian Revolution? Let us concede this (although I am not so sure of the reality of these certainties now so generously attributed to the credulous revolutionaries of yesteryear). This is no reason to forget the (often dearly paid) lessons of past defeats and the negative evidence of past setbacks. Those who thought they could ignore state power and its conquest have often been its victims: they didn't want to take power, so power took them. And those who thought they could dodge it, avoid it, get around it, invest it or circumvent it without taking it have too often been thrashed by it. The process-like force of 'defetishisation' has not been enough to save them.

Even 'Leninists' (which ones?), Holloway says, no longer know (how to change the world). But did they ever, beginning with Lenin himself, claim to possess this doctrinaire knowledge that Holloway attributes to them? History is more complicated than that. In politics there can only be one kind of strategic knowledge: a conditional, hypothetical kind of knowledge, 'a strategic hypothesis' drawn from past experiences and serving as a plumb line, in the absence of which action disperses without attaining any results. The necessity of a hypothesis in no way prevents us from knowing that future experiences will always have their share of unprecedented, unexpected aspects, obliging us to correct it constantly. Renouncing any claim to dogmatic knowledge is thus not a sufficient reason to start from scratch and ignore the past, as long as we guard against the conformism that always threatens tradition (even revolutionary tradition). While waiting for new founding experiences, it would in fact be imprudent to frivolously forget what two centuries of struggles – from June 1848 to the Chilean and Indonesian counter-revolutions, by way of the Russian Revolution, the German tragedy and the Spanish Civil War – have so painfully taught us.

Until today there has never been a case of relations of domination not being torn asunder under the shock of revolutionary crises: strategic time is not the smooth time of the minute hand of a clock, but a jagged time whose pace is set by sudden accelerations and abrupt decelerations. At these critical moments forms of dual power have always emerged, posing the question 'who will beat whom'. In the end no crisis has ever turned out well from the point of view of the oppressed without resolute intervention by a political force (whether you call it a party or a movement) carrying a project forward and capable of taking decisions and decisive initiatives.

We have lost our certainties, Holloway repeats like the hero played by Yves Montand in a bad movie (*Les Routes du Sud*, with a script by Jorge Semprun). No doubt we must learn to do without them. But wherever there is a struggle (whose outcome is uncertain by definition) there is a clash of opposing wills and convictions, which are not certainties but guides to action, subject to the always-possible falsifications of practice. We must say yes to the 'openness to uncertainty' that Holloway demands, but no to a leap into a strategic void!

In the depths of this void the only possible outcome of the crisis is the event itself, but an event without actors, a purely mythical event, cut off from its historical conditions, which pulls loose from the realm of political struggle only to tumble into the domain of theology. This is what Holloway calls to mind when he invites his readers to think 'of an anti-politics of events rather than a politics of organisation'.[29] The transition from a politics of organisation to an anti-politics of the event can find its way, he says, by means of the experiences of May '68, the Zapatista rebellion or the wave of demonstrations against capitalist globalisation. These 'events are flashes against fetishism, festivals of the non-subordinate, carnivals of the oppressed'.[30] Is carnival the form, found at long last, of the post-modern revolution?

Remembrance of subjects past

Will it be a revolution – a carnival – without actors? Holloway reproaches 'identity politics' with the 'fixation of identities': the appeal to what one is supposed to 'be' always in his eyes implies a crystallisation of identity, whereas there are no grounds for distinguishing between good and bad identities. Identities only take on meaning in a specific situation and in a transitory way: claiming a Jewish identity did not have the same significance in Nazi Germany that it does today in Israel. Referring to a lovely text in which Sub-Commandante Marcos champions the multiplicity of overlapping and superimposed identities under the anonymity of the famous ski-mask, Holloway goes so far as to present Zapatismo as an 'explicitly anti-identitarian' movement.[31] The crystallisation of identity by contrast is for him the antithesis of reciprocal recognition, community, friendship and love, and a form of selfish solipsism. While identification and classificatory definition are weapons in the disciplinary arsenal of power, the dialectic expresses the deeper meaning of non-identity: 'We, the non-identical, fight against this identification. The struggle against capital is the struggle against identification. It is not the struggle for an alternative identity.'[32] Identifying comes down to thinking based on being, while thinking based on doing and acting is identifying and denying identification in one and the same movement.[33] Holloway's critique thus presents itself as an 'an assault on identity',[34] a refusal to let oneself be defined, classified and identified. We are not what they think, and the world is not what they claim.

What point is there then in continuing to say 'we'? What can this royal 'we' in fact refer to? It cannot designate any great transcendental subject (Humanity, Woman, or the Proletariat). Defining the working class would mean reducing it to the status of an object of capital and stripping it of its subjectivity. The quest for a positive subject must thus be renounced: 'Class, like the state, like money, like capital, must be understood as process. Capitalism is the ever renewed generation of class, the ever renewed classification of people.'[35] The approach is hardly new (for those of us who have never looked for a substance in the concept of class struggle, but only for a relation). It is this process of 'formation', always begun anew and always incomplete, that E.P. Thompson brilliantly studied in his book on the English working class.

But Holloway goes further. While the working class can constitute a sociological notion, there does not for him exist any such thing as a revolutionary class. Our 'struggle is not to establish a new identity or composition, but to intensify anti-identity. The crisis of identity is a liberation':[36] it will free a plurality of forms of resistance and a multiplicity of screams. This multiplicity cannot be subordinated to the a priori unity of a mythical Proletariat; for from the standpoint of doing and acting we are this that and many other things as well, depending on the situation and the shifting conjuncture. Do all identifications, however fluid and variable, play an equivalent role in determining the terms and stakes of the struggle? Holloway fails to ask (himself) the question. Taking his distance from Negri's fetishism of the multitude, he expresses fear only when the unresolved strategic enigma breaks through: he worries that emphasising multiplicity while forgetting the underlying unity of the relationships of power can lead to a loss of political perspective, to the point that emancipation then becomes inconceivable. So, noted.

The spectre of anti-power

In order to get out of this impasse and solve the strategic enigma posed by the sphinx of capital, Holloway's last word is 'anti-power': 'This book is an exploration of the absurd and shadowy world of anti-power.'[37] He uses the distinction developed by Negri between 'power-to' ('*potentia*') and 'power-over' ('*potestas*') for his own purposes. The goal he advocates is to free power-to from power-over, doing from work, and subjectivity from objectification. If power-over sometimes comes 'out of the barrel of a gun', this he thinks is not the case with power-to. The very notion of anti-power still depends on power-over. Yet the struggle to liberate power-to is not the struggle to construct a counter-power, but rather an anti-power, something that is radically different from power-over. Concepts of revolution that focus on the taking of power are typically centred on the notion of counter-power.

55

Thus the revolutionary movement has too often been constructed 'as a mirror image of power, army against army, party against party'. Holloway defines anti-power by contrast as 'the dissolution of power-over' in the interest of 'the emancipation of power-to'.[38] What is Holloway's strategic conclusion (or anti-strategic conclusion, if strategy as well is too closely linked to power-over)? 'It should now be clear that power cannot be taken, for the simple reason that power is not possessed by any particular person or institution' but rather lies 'in the fragmentation of social relations'.[39] Having reached this sublime height, Holloway contentedly contemplates the volume of dirty water being bailed out of the bathtub, but he worries about how many babies are being thrown out with it. The perspective of power to the oppressed has indeed given way to an indefinable, ungraspable anti-power, about which we are told only that it is everywhere and nowhere, like the centre of Pascale's circumference. Does the spectre of anti-power thus haunt the bewitched world of capitalist globalisation? It is on the contrary very much to be feared that the multiplication of 'anti's' (the anti-power of an anti-revolution made with an anti-strategy) might in the end be no more than a paltry rhetorical stratagem, whose ultimate result is to disarm the oppressed (theoretically and practically) without for all that breaking the iron grasp of capital and its domination.

An imaginary Zapatismo

Philosophically, Holloway finds in Deleuze and Foucault's works a representation of power as a 'multiplicity of relationships of forces', rather than as a binary relationship. This ramified power can be distinguished from the state based on sovereign prerogatives and its apparatuses of domination. The approach is hardly a new one. As early as the 1970s, Foucault's *Discipline and Punish* and *History of Sexuality Volume One* influenced certain critical reinterpretations of Marx.[40] Holloway's problematic, often close to Negri's, nonetheless diverges from it when he reproaches Negri with limiting himself to a radical democratic theory founded on the counterposition of constituent power to institutionalised power: a still binary logic of a clash of titans between the monolithic might of capital (Empire with a capital letter) and the monolithic might of the Multitude (also with a capital letter).

Holloway's main reference point is the Zapatista experience, whose theoretical spokesperson he appoints himself. His Zapatismo seems however to be imaginary, or even mythical, inasmuch as it takes hardly any account of the real contradictions of the political situation, the real difficulties and obstacles that the Zapatistas have encountered since the uprising of 1 January 1994. Limiting himself to the level of discourse, Holloway does not even try to identify the reasons for the Zapatistas' failure to develop an urban base.

The innovative character of Zapatista communications and thought are undeniable. In his lovely book *The Zapatista Spark* Jérôme Baschet analyses the Zapatistas' contributions with sensitivity and subtlety, without trying to deny their uncertainties and contradictions.[41] Holloway by contrast tends to take their rhetoric literally.

Limiting ourselves to the issues of power and counter-power, civil society and the vanguard, there can scarcely be any doubt that the Chiapas uprising of 1 January 1994 ('the moment when the critical forces were once more set in motion', says Baschet) should be seen as part of the renewal of resistance to neoliberal globalisation that has since become unmistakable, from Seattle to Genoa by way of Porto Alegre. This moment is also a strategic 'ground zero', a moment of critical reflection, stocktaking and questioning, in the aftermath of the 'short twentieth century' and the Cold War (presented by Marcos as a sort of third world war). In this particular transitional situation, the Zapatista spokespeople insist that 'Zapatismo does not exist' (Marcos) and that it has 'neither a line nor recipes'. They say they do not want to capture the state or even take power, but that they aspire to 'to something only a bit more difficult: a new world'. What we need to take is ourselves, Holloway translates. Yet the Zapatistas do reaffirm the necessity of a 'new revolution': there can be no change without a break. This is thus the hypothesis that Holloway has developed of a revolution without taking power. Looking at the Zapatistas' formulations more closely however, they are more complex and ambiguous than they first seem. One can see in them first of all a form of self-criticism of the armed movements of the 1960s and '70s, of military verticalism, of the readiness to give orders to social movements, and of caudilloist deformations. At this level Marcos' texts and the EZLN communiqués mark a salutary turning point, renewing the hidden tradition of 'socialism from below' and popular self-emancipation.

The goal is not to take power for oneself (the party, army or vanguard) but rather to contribute to turning power over to the people, while emphasising the difference between the state apparatuses strictly speaking and relationships of power that are more deeply embedded in social relations (beginning with the social division of labour among individuals, between the sexes, between intellectual and manual workers, etc.). At a second, tactical level, the Zapatista discourse on power points to a discursive strategy. Conscious as they are that the conditions for overthrowing the central government and ruling class are far from being met on the scale of a country with a 3000-kilometre-long border with the American imperial giant, the Zapatistas choose not to want what they cannot achieve in any event. This is making a virtue of necessity so as to position themselves for a war of attrition and a lasting duality of power, at least on a regional scale.

At a third, strategic level, the Zapatista discourse comes down to denying the importance of the question of power in order simply to demand the organisation of civil society. This theoretical position reproduces for them the dichotomy between civil society (social movements) and political (particularly electoral) institutions. Civil society is in their eyes dedicated to acting as pressure (lobbying) groups on institutions that civil society is resigned to being unable to change.

Situated in not very favourable national, regional and international relationships of forces, the Zapatista discourse plays on all these different registers, while the Zapatistas' practice navigates skilfully among all the rocks. This is absolutely legitimate – as long as we do not take pronouncements that are founded on strategic calculations, while claiming to rise above them, too literally. The Zapatistas themselves know full well that they are playing for time; they can relativise the question of power in their communiqués, but they do know that the actually existing power of the Mexican bourgeoisie and army, and even the 'Northern colossus', will not fail to crush the indigenous rebellion in Chiapas if they get the chance, just as the US and Colombian state are now trying to crush the Colombian guerrillas. By painting a quasi-angelic picture of Zapatismo, at the cost of taking his distance from any concrete history or politics, Holloway is sustaining dangerous illusions. Not only does the Stalinist counter-revolution play no role in his balance sheet of the twentieth century, but also, in his work as in François Furet's, all history results from correct or incorrect ideas. He thus allows himself a balance sheet in which all the books are already closed, since in his eyes both experiences have failed, the reformist experience as well as the revolutionary. The verdict is to say the least hasty, wholesale (and crude), as if there existed only two symmetrical experiences, two competing and equally failed approaches; and as if the Stalinist regime (and its other avatars) resulted from the 'revolutionary experience' rather than the Thermidorian counter-revolution. This strange historic logic would make it just as possible to proclaim that the French Revolution has failed, the American Revolution has failed, etc.[42]

We will have to dare to go far beyond ideology and plunge into the depths of historical experience in order to pick up once more the thread of a strategic debate that has been buried under the sheer weight of accumulated defeats. On the threshold of a world that is in some ways wholly new to us, in which the new straddles the old, it is better to acknowledge what we do not know and stay open to new experiences to come than to theorise our powerlessness by minimising the obstacles that lie ahead.

First published by *Historical Materialism*:
http://www.historicalmaterialism.net

Appendix: Screams and Spit

(Twelve Comments Plus One More, to Continue the Debate with John Holloway): [43]

(i) 'Spit on history', John Holloway retorts.[44] Why not? But on which history? For him, apparently, there is only one history, a one-way history, the history of oppression that even contaminates the struggle of the oppressed. As if history and memory were not themselves battlefields. As if a history of the oppressed – often an oral history (history of the exploited, women's history, gay history, the history of colonised peoples) – did not also exist, just as we can conceive of a theatre of the oppressed or a politics of the oppressed.

(ii) For Holloway, history is 'the great excuse for not thinking'. Does he mean that it is impossible to think historically? And, then, what do we mean by 'thinking'? – An old question, that, always getting in the way.

(iii) Spit 'also on the concept of Stalinism', which absolves us of the 'need to blame ourselves' and constitutes a convenient 'fig-leaf, protecting our innocence'. No one today imagines that the revolution of the 1920s, luminous and immaculate, can be counterposed to the dark 1930s on which we can dump every sin. No one has emerged unscathed from the 'century of extremes'. Everyone needs methodically to examine their conscience, including us. But is this sufficient reason to erase the discontinuities that Michel Foucault was so fond of? To establish a strict genealogical continuity between the revolutionary event and the bureaucratic counter-revolution? To pronounce an evenly balanced verdict of 'guilty' on both the victors and vanquished, the executioners and their victims? This is not a moral question but a political one. It determines whether it is possible to 'continue' or 'begin anew'. The darkness of non-history, in which all cats are grey (without, for all, that catching the tiniest mouse) is the preferred landscape for neoliberals and repentant Stalinists to hold their reunions, hurriedly wiping out the traces of their past without thinking about this past that makes it so hard for them to pass.

(iv) 'Spit on history because there is nothing so reactionary as the cult of the past'; So be it. But who is talking about a cult? Does tradition weigh like a nightmare on the brain of the living? Definitely. But what tradition? Where does this tradition in the singular come from, in which so many contrary traditions vanish away? By contrast, Walter Benjamin, whom Holloway cites so eagerly (appositely or not), demands that we rescue tradition from the conformism that always threatens it. This distinction is essential.

(v) 'Break history. Du passé faisons table rase'.[45] The song rings out proudly. But the politics of the blank page (which Chairman Mao was so fond of) and the blank slate evokes some rather disquieting precedents. Its most consistent advocate was none other than a certain Pol Pot. Gilles Deleuze speaks more wisely when he says, 'We always begin again from the middle.'

(vi) 'Spit on history'? Nietzsche himself, certainly the most virulent critic of historical reason and the myth of progress, was subtler.[46] He did, admittedly, recommend learning to forget in order to be able to act. He took exception to any history that would be 'a kind of conclusion to living and a final reckoning for humanity'. But, while he implacably denounced 'monumental history', 'antiquarian history', 'excess of historical culture' and the 'supersaturation of an age in history', and history as such as 'a disguised theology', he maintained, nonetheless, that 'living requires the services of history': "To be sure, we need history. But we need it in a manner different from the way in which the spoilt idler in the garden of knowledge uses it . . . for life and action, not for a comfortable turning away from life and action..." Nietzsche thus defended the necessity of a 'critical history'. At least he claimed to counter 'the effects of history', not with a politics of emancipation, but, rather, with an aesthetic: the 'powers of art, or the "super-historical"... powers which divert the gaze from what is developing back... to art and religion'. Myth against history?

(vii) 'We live in a world of Monsters of our own creation'. While commodities, money, capital and the state are fetishes, they are not 'mere illusions, they are real illusions'. Exactly. What follows from this, in practical terms? That abolishing these illusions requires abolishing the social relations that make them necessary and fabricate them? Or, as Holloway suggests, that we must be content with a fetish strike: 'Capital exists because we create it... If we do not create it tomorrow, it will cease to exist'? In the aftermath of 1968, there were Maoists who claimed that 'driving out the cop' in our heads would be enough to get rid of the real cops too. Yet the real cops are still with us (more than ever), and the tyranny of the ego is still secure even in the best regulated minds. So would refusing to create capital suffice to lift its spells? Magical behaviour (conjuring away in our imaginations an imaginary despot) would only bring about a liberation which is just as imaginary. Abolishing the conditions of fetishism in reality means overthrowing the despotism of the market and the power of private property and breaking the state that ensures the conditions of social reproduction.

(viii) No doubt, this is all an old story. But where are the new stories? The new must always be made (at least in part) with the bricks of the old. Holloway defines the revolution as 'the breaking of tradition, the discarding of history . . . the smashing of the clock and the concentration of time into a moment of unbearable intensity'. Here, he is recycling the imagery that Benjamin used in describing the rebels in 1830 who fired on the faces of public clocks. The symbolic destruction of the image of time still confuses the fetish of temporality with the social relationship on which it rests: the 'wretched' measurement of abstract labour time.

(ix) Holloway blots out with his spit the criticisms that Atilio Boron, Alex Callinicos, Guillermo Almeyra and I have made of his work. He reproaches us with envisaging history as 'something unproblematic', instead of opening it up to theoretical questions. This is a gratuitous accusation, backed up neither with arguments nor with serious evidence. All of us have, on the contrary, devoted much of our work to interrogating, revising, deconstructing and reconstructing our historical worldview.[47] History is like power; you cannot ignore it. You can refuse to take power, but then it will take you. You can throw history out the door, but it will kick over the traces and come back in through the window.

(x) There is 'something fundamentally wrong with the power-centred concept of revolution'. But what? Foucault passed this way a long time ago. As I have already mentioned, more than twenty-five years ago I wrote a book entitled La Révolution et le Pouvoir ('The Revolution and Power'), around the idea that the state can be broken but the 'relations of power' must still be undone (or deconstructed). This is not a new issue. It reached us by way of libertarian traditions and May '68, among others. Why, if not out of ignorance, does Holloway make a show of radically innovating (still making a clean sweep) instead of situating himself in discussions that have... a (long) history!

(xi) 'The accumulation of struggle is an incremental view of revolution', says Holloway. It is a positive movement, whereas the anticapitalist movement 'must be a negative movement'. Criticising illusions of progress, the stockbroker spirit, Penelopes weaving their electoral skeins (stitch by stitch, link by link), interest piled on interest, and the ineluctable march of history as it triumphs over regrettable skids, detours and delays – all this criticism itself belongs to an old tradition (represented in France by Georges Sorel and Charles Péguy, who had so much influence on Benjamin). But, just the same, is the absolute interruption of a scream without a past or a sequel enough to outweigh the continuities of historical time? Benjamin takes exception to the homogenous, empty time of the mechanics of progress, and with it to the notion of an evanescent present, a simple, evanescent hyphen, absolutely determined by the past and irresistibly aspiring to a predestined future. In Benjamin's work, by contrast, the present becomes the central category of a strategic temporality: each present is thus invested with a feeble messianic power of reshuffling the cards of past and future, giving the vanquished of yesterday and forever their chance, and rescuing tradition from conformism.[48] Yet, for all that, this present is not detached from historical time. As in Blanqui's work, it maintains relations with past events, not relations of causality, but, rather, relations of astral attraction and constellation. It is in this sense that, to use Benjamin's definitive formulation, from now on, politics trumps history.

(xii) 'Using History as a pretext', Holloway says, we want to 'pour new struggles into old methods': 'Let the new forms of struggle flourish.' Just because we are constantly welcoming a portion of newness, history(!) exists rather than some divine or mercantile eternity. But the historical dialectic of old and new is subtler than any binary or Manichean opposition between old and new, including in the methodological sense. Yes, let the new flourish; do not give in to routine and habit; stay open to surprise and astonishment. This is all useful advice. But how, by what standard, can we evaluate the new if we lose all memory of the old? Novelty, like antiquity, is always a relative notion.

Screaming and spitting do not amount to thinking. Still less to doing politics.

Notes

1 Robert Michels, Political Parties: A Sociological Study of the Oligarchical Tendencies of Modern Democracy, trans. by Eden Paul (et al.), New York: Free Press, 1987.

2 See Michael Löwy, Redemption and Utopia, London: Athlone, 1992.

3 See in particular Michael Hardt and Antonio Negri, Empire, Cambridge MA: Harvard University Press, 2000, and John Holloway, Change the World without Taking Power, London: Pluto Press, 2002 (Spanish translation: Cambiar el Mundo sin Tomar el Poder, Buenos Aires: Herramienta, 2002).

4 It is in fact striking in this respect to observe how much more respectful (and even ceremonious) and how much less critical this tendency is of its heritage than heterodox neo-Marxism is when it turns 'back to Marx'.

5 See Daniel Bensaïd, La Discordance des temps, Paris: Editions de la Passion, 1995 – English version Marx for Our Times, Verso 2003; Résistances: Essai de Tauplologie Générale, Paris: Fayard, 2001; articles in ContreTemps no. 2 and the Italian journal Erre no. 1 (on the notion of the multitude); and finally a contribution that will be published by Verso in an English-language anthology.

6 Citations from John Holloway, Change the World Without Taking Power, London: Pluto Press, 2002, p. 8.

7 Holloway 2002, p. 164.

8 Holloway 2002, p. 19.

9 Holloway 2002, p. 73.

10 Holloway 2002, p. 94.

11 Holloway 2002, p. 96.

12 See the debates published in ContreTemps no. 3.

13 Holloway 2002, p. 210.

14 Holloway 2002, p. 54, quoting Marx 1966, p. 830.

15 Holloway 2002, p. 74.

16 Holloway 2002, p. 140.

17 Holloway 2002, p. 76.

18 Holloway 2002, p. 90.

19 Holloway 2002, p. 182.

20 Holloway hardly ventures at all to examine this Copernican revolution critically. Yet a quarter of a century later an evaluation is possible, if only to avoid repeating the same theoretical illusions and the same practical errors while dressing up the same discourse in new terminological clothes. See on this subject Maria Turchetto's contribution on 'the disconcerting trajectory of Italian autonomism' in Dictionnaire Marx Contemporain, Jacques Bidet and Eustache Kouvélakis eds., Paris: PUF, 2001; and Steve Wright, Storming Heaven: Class Composition

and Struggle in Italian Autonomist Marxism, London: Pluto Press, 2002.

21 Jean-Marie Vincent, Fétichisme et Société, Paris: Anthropos, 1973.

22 Stavros Tombazos, Les Temps du Capital, Paris: Cahiers des Saisons, 1976; Alain Bihr, La Reproduction du Capital (2 vols.), Lausanne: Page 2, 2001.

23 Holloway 2002, p. 210.

24 Holloway 2002, p. 140.

25 V.I. Lenin, 'What Is to Be Done?: Burning Questions of Our Movement', in Collected Works vol. 5, Moscow: Progress Publishers, 1961, pp. 384, 422; and see Daniel Bensaïd, 'Leaps! Leaps! Leaps!', in International Socialism no. 95, Summer 2002.

26 Holloway 2002, p. 139.

27 Holloway 2002, p. 20.

28 Holloway 2002, p. 215.

29 Holloway 2002, p. 214.

28 Holloway 2002, p. 215.

29 Holloway 2002, p. 214.

30 Holloway 2002, p. 215.

31 Holloway 2002, p. 64.

32 Holloway 2002, p. 100.

33 Holloway 2002, p. 102.

34 Holloway 2002, p. 106.

35 Holloway 2002, p. 142.

36 Holloway 2002, p. 212.

37 Holloway 2002, p. 38.

38 Holloway 2002, p. 37.

39 Holloway 2002, p. 72.

40 This was the case with many books including one of my own, with the significant title La Révolution et le Pouvoir (The Revolution and Power, Paris: Stock, 1976), whose introductory note (which some comrades held against me) read, 'The first proletarian revolution gave its response to the problem of the state. Its degeneration has left us with the problem of power. The state must be destroyed and its machinery broken. Power must be pulled apart in its institutions and its underground anchorages. How can the struggle through which the proletariat constitutes itself as a ruling class contribute to this process, despite the apparent contradiction? We must once more take up the analysis of the crystallisations of power within capitalist society, trace their resurgence within the bureaucratic counter-revolution, and look in the struggle of the exploited classes for the tendencies that can enable the socialisation and withering away of power to win out over the statification of society.'[7]

41 Jérôme Baschet, L'Etincelle Zapatiste: Insurrection Indienne et Résistance Planétaire, Paris: Denoël, 2002.

42 See Atilio Boron's article 'La Selva y la Polis', OSAL (Buenos Aires), June 2001, and Isidro Cruz Bernal's article in Socialismo o Barabarie (Buenos Aires), no. 11, May 2002. While expressing their sympathy and solidarity with the Zapatista resistance, they warn against the temptation to base a new model on it while masking its theoretical and strategic impasses.

43 John Holloway responded to the above piece in ContreTemps no. with an article entitled 'Drive Your Cart and Your Plough Over the Bones of the Dead', Holloway 2004. The following is Bensaïd's riposte.

44 Quotes from Holloway 2004.

45 In French in Holloway's text: 'Make a clean sweep of the past' (translator's note).

46 Quotes from Nietzsche 2004.

47 See, for example, Bensaïd 2002b, and Callinicos 1995 and 2004.

48 On Benjamin, see Bensaïd 1990.

References

Baschet, Jérôme 2002, L'Etincelle zapatiste: insurrection indienne et résistance planétaire, Paris: Denoël.

Bensaïd, Daniel 1976, La Révolution et le Pouvoir, Paris: Stock.

Bensaïd, Daniel 1990, Walter Benjamin sentinelle messianique: à la gauche du possible, Paris: Plon.

Bensaïd, Daniel 1995, La Discordance des temps, Paris: Editions de la Passion.

Bensaïd, Daniel 2001a, Résistances: Essai de taupologie générale, Paris: Fayard.

Bensaïd, Daniel 2001b, 'Le nouveau désordre impérial', Contretemps, 2: 9-20.

Bensaïd, Daniel 2001c, 'Giovanni Arrighi et le "long XXe" siècle', Contretemps, 2: 144-6.

Bensaïd, Daniel 2002a, 'Leaps! Leaps! Leaps!', International Socialism, 95: 73-86.

Bensaïd, Daniel 2002b, Marx for Our Times: Adventures and Misadventures of a Critique, Translated by Gregory Elliott, London: Verso.

Bensaïd, Daniel forthcoming (a), 'Ventriloquist Multitudes', Historical Materialism.

Bensaïd, Daniel forthcoming (b), in The Philosophy of Antonio Negri: Resistance in Practice, Volume 2, edited by Timothy S Murphy & Abdul-Karim Mustapha, London: Pluto Press.

Bernal, Isidro Cruz 2002, 'Elegante manera de hacerse el distraído', Socialismo o Barbarie, 11.

Bihr, Alain 2001, La Reproduction du Capital (2 vols.), Lausanne: Page 2.

Boron, Atilio 2001, 'La Selva y la Polis: Reflexiones en torno a la teoría política del zapatismo', OSAL, 4: 177-86

Callinicos, Alex 1995, Theories and Narratives: Reflections on the Philosophy of History, Cambridge: Polity.

Callinicos, Alex 2004, Making History: Agency, Structure, and Change in Social Theory, Second Revised Edition, HM Book Series, Leiden: Brill Academic Press.

Hardt, Michael and Antonio Negri 2000, Empire, Cambridge, MA.: Harvard University Press.

Holloway, John 2002, Change the World without Taking Power, London: Pluto Press (Spanish translation: Cambiar el Mundo sin Tomar el Poder, Buenos Aires: Herramienta, 2002).

Holloway, John 2004, 'Drive Your Cart and Your Plough Over the Bones Of the Dead', Lenin, Vladimir Ilych 1961 (1902), 'What Is to Be Done?: Burning Questions of Our Movement' in Collected Works, Volume 5, Moscow: Progress Publishers.

Löwy, Michael 1992, Redemption and Utopia, London: Athlone.

Marx, Karl 1966 (1894), Capital, Volume III, London: Lawrence and Wishart.

Michels, Robert 1987, Political Parties: A Sociological Study of the Oligarchical Tendencies of Modern Democracy, New York: Free Press.

Nietzsche, Friedrich 2004 (1873), 'The Use and Abuse of History for Life', translated by Ian Johnston.

Tombazos, Stavros 1996, Les Temps du Capital, Paris: Cahiers des Saisons.

Turchetto, Maria 2001, 'De "l'ouvrier masse" à l'entrepreneurialité commune': la trajectoire déconcertante de l'operaisme italien', in Dictionnaire Marx Contemporain, edited by Jacques Bidet and Eustache Kouvélakis, Paris: PUF.

Vincent, Jean-Marie 1973, Fétichisme et société, Paris: Anthropos.

Wright, Steve 2002. Storming Heaven: Class Composition and Struggle in Italian Autonomist Marxism, London: Pluto Press.

John Holloway
"Drive your cart and your plough over the bones of the dead"

2005

"Drive your cart and your plough over the bones of the dead." [2]

That is my response to those[3] who criticise my book[4] for being anti-historical. This article is not a defence of the book: I can think of nothing more boring. We need to drive the argument forwards, not backwards. Books, like revolutions, cannot be defended: they go forward or they die.

1 Drive your Cart

Spit on history. History is the history of oppression told by the oppressors, a history from which oppression conveniently disappears, a history of Heroes, of Great Men.

Spit on history. History, even our history, is a history in which the struggle against oppression is invaded by the categories of the oppressors, so that it too becomes the history of Heroes, of Great Men, of Marx, Engels, Lenin, Trotsky, Stalin, Mao.

Spit on history, because it is the great alibi of the Left, the great excuse for not thinking. Make any theoretical or political argument about revolution and the response of the Revolutionary Left is to bring you back to 1902, to 1905, to 1917, to 1921. History becomes a whirlpool, sucking you into the details of lives long dead. Present political differences become translated into disputes about the details of what happened in Kronstadt over eighty years ago. Anything to avoid thinking about the present, anything to avoid assuming the terrible responsibility that the future of the world depends on us and not on Lenin or Trotsky.

Spit on history, spit on Stalin (that is easy), but spit also on the concept of Stalinism. Stalinism is the greatest alibi, the greatest excuse for not thinking, for an important part of the revolutionary left. "Look at what happened in the Soviet Union, how the great Bolshevik Revolution led to tyranny and misery." "Yes," they reply, "Stalinism." History becomes a substitute for critical and self-critical thought. Between Bolshevik revolution and Soviet tyranny a figure is introduced to relieve us revolutionaries from responsibility. If we have Stalin to blame, then we do not need to blame ourselves, we do not need to be critical or self-critical, we do not need to think. Above all, we do not need to think that perhaps there was something wrong with the Leninist project of conquering power. Stalin becomes a fig-leaf, protecting our innocence, hiding our nakedness.

Spit, then, on Stalinism. When people criticise my book for being anti-historical, what they mean in most cases (not all) is that, by not mentioning Stalin, the book takes away this fig-leaf, exposes our complicity. "Revolutions focussed on the taking of power have led to disaster, therefore we must rethink what revolution means" is what I argue. "No," they reply, "it is true that these revolutions have led to disaster, but this was because of history, because of Stalinism; we do not need to rethink anything." This history, of course, is a peculiar history: it paints out of the picture those who said from the very beginning that the state-centred concept of revolution was flawed: not one of the critics mentions the name of Pannekoek.

Spit on history because there is nothing so reactionary as the cult of the past.[5] "The tradition of all the dead generations weighs like a nightmare on the brain of the living", says Marx. Revolutionary thought means shaking off that nightmare, waking up to our own responsibilities. Self-determination – communism, in other words, both as movement and as aim – is emancipation from the nightmare of tradition.

Spit on history because "an ideology of history has one purpose only: to prevent people from making history".[6]

2 Contre Temps

Revolution is the shooting of clocks, the breaking of time.[7]

The rule of value is the rule of duration. The breaking of duration is the pivot of revolutionary thought and action.

In capitalism, that which we make stands against us. Like Frankenstein"s Creature, it stands outside us and denies the creative doing which gave it existence."A commodity is in the first place an object outside us", as Marx says at the beginning of Capital.[8] As an object outside us, it stands against us, presents itself as having an existence of its own, a duration independent of our doing. Capitalism is the rule of things that we have made and which deny their origin and continuing dependence on our doing.

We live in a world of Monsters of our own creation which have turned against us. They stand there, apparently independent of us, oppressing us: Commodity, Money, Capital, State and so on. They were there yesterday, they were there a hundred years ago, two hundred years ago. It seems certain that they will be there tomorrow. They are oppressing us, dehumanising us, killing us. How can we free ourselves, how can we get rid of them? They have been there for so long, their existence seems everlasting. How can we possibly escape?

"Wake up," says Papa Marx, "it"s just a nightmare. These Monsters are an illusion." We wake up and the Monsters are gone, we see that they were not everlasting, their duration is dissolved.

But no. It is not as simple as that. Maybe our vision of Marx was just a dream, because when we open our eyes the Monsters are still there, and more aggressive than ever, attacking Iraq, closing factories, reforming universities in their own image, subordinating every aspect of our lives to their domination, turning us into little monsters ourselves, so that we run around worshipping Commodity, Money, Capital and State.

The nightmare continues. Yet Marx was right, it is a nightmare, and the Monsters are illusions. But they are not mere illusions, they are real illusions. They are what Marx calls "fetishes". But what is a real illusion? On that hangs the meaning of revolution.

The Monsters seem everlasting. How do we break their duration?

If we take the Monsters as what they appear to be, as creatures independent of ourselves, then the only possibility of defeating them is by matching our strength against theirs, our power against theirs.

That is not Marx"s approach. Marx says"The Monsters are not what they appear to be. We must criticise them. The Monsters exist because we made them.""I beg your pardon", we say,"can you say that again please?"And Marx replies"The Monsters are not what they appear to be. We must criticise them. The Monsters exist because we make them.""But that is not what you said the first time", we say,"the first time you said "made", the second time you said "make". Which do you mean?" But Marx does not reply – he has been dead for over a hundred years. We are left to assume our own responsibility.

Commodity, money, capital, the state: all these are own creations. That is the core of Marx"s method, the centre of his argument in Capital.[9]

We create the monsters which oppress us. But, even taking this as a starting point, there is still a huge question. When we create these fetishes (these social relations that exist as things), are we like Dr. Frankenstein creating a monster that acquires an existence independent from us? Or are we creating fetishes that only appear to acquire an independent existence, but which depend for their existence on our constant re-creation? Does capital exist because we created it, or does it exist because we constantly recreate it?[10] In the former case, revolution means destroying the monster that we have created. In the second case, revolution means ceasing to create the monster. The implications of this distinction for how we think about revolution and revolutionary organisation are probably enormous.

Capital exists because we create it. We created it yesterday (and every day for the last two hundred years or so). If we do not create it tomorrow, it will cease to exist. Its existence depends on the constant repetition of the process of exploitation (and of all the social processes that make exploitation possible). It is not like Frankenstein"s creature. It does not have an existence independent of our doing. It does not have a duration, a durable independent existence. It only appears to have a duration. The same is true of all the derivative forms of capital (state, money, etc.). The continuity of these monsters (these forms of social relations) is not something that exists independent of us: their continuity is a continuity that is constantly generated and re-generated by our doing. The fact that we have reasons for generating capital does not alter the fact that capital depends for its existence from one day to the next, from one moment to the next, on our act of creation. Capital depends upon us: that is the ray of hope in a world that seems so black.

With this, the clock explodes. If capital"s existence depends on our creation of it, it becomes clear that revolution is the breaking of that repeated act of creation. Revolution is the breaking of continuity, the rupture of duration, the transformation of time. The clock has tick-tick-ticked for two hundred years, telling the monstrous lie on which capitalism depends, the lie that says that one moment is the same as the last: it must tick no more. Capitalism is the establishment of continuity, of duration, of tradition, the projection of the present moment into the next, and the next, and the next. Revolution is not progress, or planning or the fulfilment of tradition or the culmination of history: it is the opposite of all that. It is the breaking of tradition, the discarding of history (its dismissal to the realm of pre-history), the smashing of the clock and the concentration of time into a moment of unbearable intensity. Communism is not five-year plans but self-determination, and self-determination is an absolute present in which no nightmare of tradition weighs upon us, in which there are no monsters. That is why Benjamin insists on the Jetztzeit (the now-moment) as the key to revolution[11], why Bloch sees communism as the pursuit of the Nunc Stans, the moment of perfect intensity,[12] why Vaneigem says that the task is to subvert history with the watchword"Act as though there were no tomorrow".[13]

Continuities existed perhaps in the past: once we project them into the future, we render revolution conceptually impossible, we defeat ourselves. Periodisation of the present is always reactionary, whether we categorise the present in terms of a long wave, or a mode of regulation, or a paradigm. Revolution depends on the opening up of every moment, so that our continued production of our own repression (if that should happen) is a matter of amazement, never, never, never to be taken for granted.

Understanding that capital depends on us for its existence from one moment to another takes us into a whole new world of perception, a whole new grammar[14], a new rhythm.[15] It seems that we are crazy, that we are entering an enchanted, perverted, topsy-turvy world. But of course it is not so: the world we are criticising, the world of capital, the world of duration, the world of identity, is the "enchanted, perverted, topsy-turvy world" (Marx 1972, 830). We are so used to this perverted world that to try to think the world from the starting point of our own doing seems insane. But we must plunge into this insanity, put our own doing in its proper place as the true sun:[16] that is our struggle.

When I say that capital depends for its existence from one moment to the next on our creation, I do not meant that getting rid of capitalism is a simple act of volition or choice. Capital is a real illusion, not a mere illusion: its independence from us is an illusion, but it is an illusion really generated by our alienated labour, by the fracturing of our social doing. The understanding that capital is produced by us, and depends for its existence from one day to the next on our production of it, does not mean that we cease to produce it. It does, however, bring us to reformulate the question of revolution, to ask how we can stop producing the domination that is destroying us. How do we break continuity, not just the continuity of their domination, but the continuity of our production of their domination? How do we break not just their tradition but our tradition as well?

Break history. Du passé faisons table rase.[17]

3 Drive your Plough

Drive your cart and your plough over the bones of the dead. Yes. First your cart: show disrespect for the dead, for they have bequeathed us a world unworthy of humanity, a world of exploitation and of mass murder in the name of democracy.

And then your plough: plough the bones of the dead into the soil of revolt. Plough their legacy of struggle into the ground to make it fertile. Honour the dead by showing them disrespect.

Do not build mausoleums, or monuments, or even put gravestones for the dead, just use their bones directly as fertiliser. The disappeared are the great heroes of communism: not just those who have been disappeared by state repression,[18] but all of those unseen, unheard people who struggled to live with dignity in a world which negates dignity, the knitters of humanity. The history we need is not so much that of the great revolutionaries, but of those who did their washing and played with their children.

The history of the invisible is a negative history, the movement of the scream of (and for) that which is not yet (the communism which is not yet, which might or might not be one day, but which exists now as movement, as longing, as not yet, as negativity). The history of the scream is not the history of a Movement, or an Institution, or of Marx-Engels-Lenin-Trotsky. And it is not a continuous history but a history of leaps and bounds and breaks and the constant search for rupture. It is, as Bloch puts it, a "hard, endangered journey, a suffering, a wandering, a going astray, a searching for the hidden homeland, full of tragic interruption, boiling, bursting with leaps, eruptions, lonely promises, discontinuously laden with the consciousness of light".[19] A history in which people break their heads against duration, a history in which time itself is always at issue.

A history of broken connections, of unresolved longings, of unanswered questions. When we turn to history, it is not to find answers, but to pick up the questions bequeathed to us by the dead. To answer these questions, the only resource we have is ourselves, our thought and our practice, now, in the present. History opens questions that lead us on to theoretical reflection.

4 Appendix: Criticising the Critics

The aim of this article has been to develop some ideas prompted by those who have criticised my book for not developing a more historical approach to the question of revolution. I do not particularly want to defend my book.[20] Perhaps the critics are right, yet I think they are wrong.

They are wrong because the history that they ask for is presented as something unproblematic. To say "there is not enough history" is rather like saying "there is not enough social science": it is meaningless, because it assumes that the categories of historical discussion are clear. It takes "history" for granted, as though there were some categorially neutral history which absolved us from the need for theoretical reflection. Vega Cantor complains of the absence of "real history": but what is this "real history" – a history of kings and queens, of working class heroes? A history of class struggle, presumably, but how do we understand class struggle? As the movement of capital"s dependence upon labour and upon the conversion of doing into labour? That is what I try to do in chapter 10 of the book, but it is difficult to even attempt to do it without a prior theoretical discussion.

The central issue is perhaps the relation between historical analysis and theoretical reflection. For me, historical analysis opens up questions, pushes us to think about those questions. Thus, the history of revolutions in the twentieth century does not demonstrate that revolutions focussed on the taking of power are doomed to failure: it suggests that there is something fundamentally wrong with the power-centred concept of revolution and that therefore we have to rethink the notion of revolution. The core of the argument is not historical but theoretical: reflection on the past thrusts us towards our own responsibility to think.

For the critics, however, history is a world not of unanswered questions but of explanations. As a result, they understand my argument as saying that history shows that power-centred revolution cannot succeed, and respond that history does not show that. Instead of seeing historical analysis leading to theoretical reflection, they push theory aside and look to history for the answers. Theoretical reflection is not important: the answers are to be found in history, they claim. Thus Bensaïd: "Il faudra bien oser aller au-delà de l"idéologie, plonger dans les profondeurs de l"expérience historique, pour renouer les fils d"un débat stratégique enseveli sous le poids des défaites accumulées."The accusation of anti-historicism (Almeyra) by these authors goes hand in hand with a dismissal of theoretical reflection. Above all, do not ask us to think: the answers are to be found in the past. Thus "Holloway, porque mira las cosas desde el cielo de la abstracción teórica, no ve la concreción política e histórica de la lucha de clases" (Almeyra). And do not ask us to think about what Marx said, that is much too extreme:"

Holloway espouses an extreme form of Marx's theory of commodity fetishism "(Callinicos). Marx is not entirely dismissed (after all, we are all Marxists, aren't we?), just shunted off into an irrelevant corner. The concept of fetishism is recognised (after all, Marx did speak of that), but then dismissed as unimportant: after all, so many people have spoken of it before, so there is nothing new there (Bensaïd). And above all, why do I approach the question of revolution theoretically, when theory has nothing at all to do with politics? That is my great mistake, according to Ernesto Manzana, who claims to take from Callinicos the insight that it is a "fundamental error" to "mix questions of politics with epistemological questions". A whole chorus of voices saying "No, please, please do not ask us to think. We have all the answers, the answers are in history, Stalinism is the explanation for the failure of past revolutions. But above all, please do not ask us to think about the meaning of revolution!"

But there is something else behind the critics' insistence on the importance of history. History, says Vega Cantor, "debe ser un punto esencial en la reconstrucción de cualquier proyecto anticapitalista que no puede, ni debe, partir de cero, pues hay todo una experiencia y una memoria históricas acumuladas". That is perhaps the core of the critics' arguments: there is an accumulation of experience of struggle, of lessons learned, of wisdom won, of forms of organisation developed.

Yet I think not. Capital accumulates. It piles surplus value upon surplus value, growing in quantity, getting bigger and bigger. Struggle against capital does not accumulate. Or perhaps it does accumulate, but then it ceases to be struggle. The accumulation of struggle is the position of the Communist Parties in 1968 who said "that is not the way to make revolution, learn from our experience". The accumulation of struggle is the (now) grey-beards of 1968 telling the protestors of today "that is not the way to make revolution, learn from our experience". The accumulation of struggle is an incremental view of revolution: "We won 1.6% of the vote in the last election: after the next we may have a few deputies, in twenty years' time we could well have thirty." The movement of accumulation is a positive movement. But our movement, the movement against capitalism is and must be a negative movement: a movement not only against capital, but against all our own practices and routines and traditions which reproduce capital. The accumulation of struggle is the accumulation of tradition, of continuity, but it is not by tradition and continuity that we will break with capitalism. Think scream, think rupture, think break. "Yes, of course," say the wise heads of tradition,"we have many years of thinking of these issues, let me explain to you what happened in 1905, and 1917, and 1921, and..." But we have already fallen asleep. "Revolution now!" we say. "Ah yes," they reply, "but first we must build the party, and be ready for the appropriate point in the next long wave." But we are already dead. We and all humanity.

No, there is no accumulation of struggle. Of memories and self-justifications and identities, perhaps. Communism is not a movement of accumulation, but of negation, of leaps and bounds and breaks. Rupture, not continuity, is the centre of revolutionary thought. Rupture, not continuity, is the centre of revolutionary practice.

The new wave of struggle makes new music, a new rhythm, a new grammar. Using History as a pretext, you would pour new struggles into old methods. Do not do it. Those methods have failed. Whatever the excuses you may find for their failure, their time has passed. Do not rub our faces in the mire of the past. Let the new forms of struggle flourish. Let us drive our cart and our plough over the bones of the dead.

References

Almeyra Guillermo (2003), El dificultoso No-Asalto al No-Cielo, Memoria no. 68.

Bartra Armando (2003), El significado de la revolución según John Holloway. Notas de lectura, Chiapas, no. 15

Benjamin Walter (1973), Theses on the Philosophy of History, in Illuminations, (New York: Schocken Books)

Bensaïd Daniel (2003), La Révolution sans le pouvoir ? A propos d_un récent livre de John Holloway, Contre Temps no. 6, pp. 45-59

Blake William (1988), The Complete Poetry and Prose of William Blake, Ed. D. Erdmann (New York: Anchor Books)

Bloch Ernst (1964), Tübinger Einleitung in die Philosophie (2 Bde) (Frankfurt: Suhrkamp)

Bloch Ernst (1986), The Principle of Hope (3 vols) (Oxford: Basil Blackwell)

Callinicos Alex (2003), How do we Deal with the State?, Socialist Review, No 272, March, pp11-13

Cruz Bernal Isidoro, Elegante manera de hacerse el distraído, Socialismo o Barbarie No 11, May 2002

Manzana Ernesto, Un buen intento con un magro resultado http//www.herramienta.com.ar/index.php

Marx Karl (1965), Capital, Vol. I (Moscow: Progress)

Marx Karl and Engels Friedrich (1975), *Marx Engels Collected Works*, Vol. 3 (London: Lawrence and Wishart)

Romero Aldo (2003), *La renovada actualidad de la Revolución (y del poder para hacerla)*, Herramienta, no. 22, 173-176

Vaneigem Raoul (1994), *The Revolution of Everyday Life* (London: Left bank Books and Rebel Press)

Vega Cantor Renan (2003), *La historia brilla por su ausencia*, Herramienta, no. 22, 191-196

Wildcat (2003), *Der Schrei und die Arbeiterklasse*, Wildcat-Zirkular Nr. 65, 48-54

Zibechi Raúl (2003), *Genealogía de la Revuelta argentina* (La Plata: Letra Libre)

Notes

1 My thanks to Alberto Bonnet, Eloína Peláez, Lars Stubbe and Sergio Tischler for their comments on an earlier draft.

2 William Blake, "Proverbs of Hell", in The Marriage of Heaven and Hell: Blake (1988) 35.

3 I have in mind particularly the critiques by Daniel Bensaïd, Renan Vega Cantor, Guillermo Almeyra, Aldo Romero, Ernesto Manzana and Isidoro Cruz Bernal. I leave aside the thoughtful critique by Armando Bartra, which also raises the question of history, for separate consideration. For the full discussion surrounding the book, see http//www.herramienta.com.ar/index.php It goes without saying that I am immensely grateful to all those who have responded to the book's invitation to discuss the issue.

4 Change the World without taking Power: the Meaning of Revolution Today, Pluto, London, 2002. French edition: Syllepse, Paris, September 2003.

5 See Vaneigem (1994) 116: "In collective as well as in individual history, the cult of the past and the cult of the future are equally reactionary. Everything which has to be built has to be built in the present."

6 Vaneigem (1994) 231.

7 Benjamin in his Theses on the Philosophy of History (Thesis XV) reports that in the July revolution "on the first evening of fighting it turned out that the clocks in towers were being fired on simultaneously and independently from several places in Paris". Benjamin (1973) 262.

8 Marx (1965), 35.

9 Much "Marxist" discussion is in fact pre-critical and in that sense pre-Marxist.

10 See the story by Borges of a man who dreams another man into existence:

11 See Benjamin"s Theses on the Philosophy of History, Theses XIV and XVIII: Benjamin (1973) 261, 263.

12 See Bloch (1964), (1986).

13 Vaneigem 116, 232.

14 This is the meeting place of autonomism and critical theory. The "Copernican inversion" of autnonomism or operaismo depends for its full force on understanding that its insight takes us into a different world of reasoning (explored most fully in the tradition of critical theory). Similarly, for critical theory to escape from its chronic pessimism, it must see that demystifying the enchanted, topsy-turvy world of capitalism means seeing doing as the driving force of society. See the helpful discussion of the book by Wildcat (2002).

15 Hardt and Negri (2000) do not see this point at all. Just the contrary: they insist on dragging the insight into capital"s dependence upon labour back into an old world of paradigms.

16 Marx, Introduction to the Contribution to the Critique of Hegel"s Philosophy of Law: Marx and Engels (1975) 176.

17 "L"Internationale" (Eugène Pottier)

18 See the declaration of HIJOS (the organisation set up by children of the dispappeared in Argentina: : "Nosotros debemos crear y reinventar un camino propio, que retome la senda que ellos marcaron y que se desvie cuando sea necesario. Como hicieron ellos, con las generaciones que los precedieron, para superarlos, para ser mejores, para aportar en serio y concretamente al cambio con el que soñaron y soñamos. Para que no se nos vaya la vida repitiendo esquemas que suenan muy contundetnes, pero que no le mueven un pelo a los dueños del poder.": Zibechi (2003), in press.

19 Bloch 1964, Vol. 2, p. 29.

20 I do not want to defend the book, but I have a special request to Daniel Bensaïd: before discussing further, please read the book again. There are so many misrepresentations (or misunderstandings) of the book in your critique that it is difficult to take it as a foundation for discussion.

From the Herramienta website: http://www.herramienta.com.ar/modules. php?op=modload&name=News&file=article&sid=169

77

Michael Löwy
Review of Change the World without Taking Power *

2005

John Holloway, Change the world without taking power. The meaning of revolution today, London, Pluto Press, 2002

This is a remarkable essay, thought-provocative and truly radical – in the original sense of the word, "going to the roots of the problems". Whatever its problems and weaknesses, it brings to the fore, in an impressive way, the critical and subversive power of negativity. Its aim is ambitious and topical : "sharpening the Marxist critique of capitalism".

One of the best section of the book is the first one, *The Scream*. This few pages are among the most powerful and moving in revolutionary thought that I have red in the last years. His basic assumption is that "we need no promise of a happy-ending to justify our rejection of a world we feel to be wrong". Faced with the mutilation of lives by capitalism, "there arises a scream of sadness, a scream of horror, a scream of anger, a scream of refusal: NO." Our protest against the established order does not depend for its validity on any particular outcome. However, "the scream clings to the possibility of an opening, refuses to accept the closure of the possibility of radical otherness".

The key philosophical chapters of the book deal with Fetishism and Fetishisation. Creatively drawing on Marx, Lukacs and Adorno, Holloway defines fetishism as the separation of doing from done and the breaking of the collective flow of doing. He insists that fetishism is not a state that permeates the whole of society, but a process, the antagonistic movement of fetishisation against anti-fetishisation. Critical theory should then be understood as part of the movement of anti-fetishisation, part of the struggle to defend, restore and create the collective flow of doing.

This is a very insightful viewpoint, but J.H. seems to identify all form of objectivity with fetishism. For instance, he complains that in capitalism "the object constituted acquires a durable identity". Well, would a good chair produced in socialism not become "an object with a durable identity"? His refusal to distinguish between alienation and objectivation (cf. note 22 of ch.4) – a mistake the young Lukacs did not do, inspite of his late self-criticism of 1967 – leads to a denial of the objective materiality of human products.

Another powerful argument is his criticism of 'Scientific Marxism', i.e. of those theories which attempt to enlist certainty to the side of socialism and claim to explain and predict historical change according to 'scientific laws': "Our struggle is inherently and profoundly uncertain. This is so because certainty is conceivable only on the basis of the reification of social relations. It is possible to speak of the 'laws of motion' of society only to the extent that social relations take the form of relations between things. (...) Revolutionary change cannot possibly be conceived as following a path of certainty, because certainty is the very negation of revolutionary change. Our struggle is a struggle against reification and therefore against certainty". This section is one of the most important of the book, and a significant contribution for a critical Marxist approach to politics.

Among the 'scientific Marxists" Holloway includes Kautsky, Lenin's *What is to be Done?* (1902) and Rosa Luxemburg's *Reform or Revolution?* (1899). However, he seems to ignore her pamphlet on *The Crisis of Social-Democracy* (1915) which represents a radical methodological break with the doctrine of scientific certainty, thanks to a decisive new formulation: the historical alternative between 'socialism or barbarism'. This essay is a real turning point in the history of Marxism, precisely because it introduces the 'principle of uncertainty' in socialist politics.

Now I come to the main bone of contention, which gives the title of the book: "changing the world without taking power". Holloway suggests at first that all attempts at revolutionary change so far failed because they were based on the paradigm of change through winning state power. However, as he aknowledges on footnote 8 from page 217, historical evidence is not enough, since all attempts to change the world without seizing power have also failed, so far. He attempts therefore to ground his claim on three theoretical arguments.

The first one is that the existing state is part of the capitalist social relations. However, as he himself writes, revolutionary Marxism is aware of such connections: its aim is not to seize the existing state, but to smash it and create a new one (p. 15). The second argument is that the state as such, whatever its social content, is a fetishised form. This is the classical anarchist argument, which Marx, to a certain extent, shared, particularly in his writings on the Paris Commune, where one can find the suggestion of a non-state form of political power. But here comes his third argument, the distinction, introduced on chapter 3, but which pervades the whole book, between power-to – the capacity to do things – and power-over – the ability to command others to do what one wishes them to do. Revolutions, according to J.H. should promote the first, and uproot the second. I must confess that I'm not persuaded by this distinction. I think that there can be no form of collective life and action of human beings without some form of 'power-over'.

Let me try to explain my objections. They have to do with the idea of democracy, a concept that hardly appears in the book, or is dismissed as a "state-defined process of electorally influenced decision making"(p. 97). I have to disagree. I believe that democracy should be a central aspect in all process of social and political decision making, and particularly in a revolutionary process – an argument remarkably presented by Rosa Luxemburg in her (fraternal) critique of the Bolsheviks (*The Russian Revolution*, 1918). Democracy means that the majority has power over the minority. Not an absolute power: it has limits, and it has to respect the dignity of the other. But still, it has power-over. This applies to all kinds of human communities, including the Zapatista villages.

For instance: in 1994, after a few weeks, the Zapatistas decided to stop shooting and to negotiate a truce. Who decided? The Zapatista villages discussed, and a majority – perhaps there was even a general consensus – decided that armed fighting should cease. The minority – if there was one, I don't know – must accept this decision, or split from the Zapatista movement. The majority had power over the minority. The villages then gave order to the commanders of the EZLN to stop fire. They had power over the commanders. And finally, the commanders themselves, according to the logic of mandar obedeciendo ('command while obeying'), obeyed the orders of the villages, and instructed the Zapatista fighters to stop shooting: they had power over them. I don't pretend this is a precise description of what happened, but it is an exemple of how democracy requires some forms of 'power-over'.

One of my main objections to Holloway's discussion on the issue of power, antipower and counterpower is its extremely abstract character. He mentions the importance of memory for resistence, but there is very little memory, very little history in his arguments, very little discussion of the merits or limits of the real historical revolutionary movements, either Marxist, Anarchist or Zapatista from 1917.

In one of the few passages were he mentions some positive historical exemples of anti-fetishism and self-determination, Holloway refers to "the Paris Commune discussed by Marx, the workers' councils theorised by Pannekoek, and the village councils of the Zapatistas"(p. 105). One can show that in each one of this exemples you have forms of democratic power requiring some form of power-over. I have already discussed the practice of the Zapatistas' village councils. What about their propositions for Mexico? Holloway's book is, to a certain extent, a brilliant comment on the well known Zapatista principle of revolutionary action : "We don't want to seize power !". But this assertion cannot be understood if it is not connected to another famous slogan of the EZLN: "Everything for all, nothing for us ! ». And if one relates both statements to the fight for democracy in Mexico, which stands high in all Zapatista pronouncements, one has the following argument : "we, the Zapatista Army, dont want to seize power in our hands; we want power to all the people, i.e. a real democracy".

In the Paris Commune one has a new form of power who wasn't any more a state, in the usual sense; but still it was a power, democratically elected by the people of Paris – a combination of direct and representative democracy – and it had power over the population, by its decrees and decisions. It had power over the National Guard, and the commanders of the Guard had power over their soldiers ("let's go and put up a barricade on Boulevard de Clichy!"). And this power, the democratic power of the Paris Commune, was literally 'seized', begining with the act of seizing the material instruments of power, the cannons of the National Guard. As for the council/communist Anton Pannekoek, he wanted "all power for the workers councils", and he saw the councils as a means for the workers "to seize power and to establish their domination over society" (I'm quoting an essay from Pannekoek from 1938).

What I feel is also lacking in J.H.'s discussion is the concept of revolutionary praxis – first formulated by Marx in the *Theses on Feuerbach* – which for me is the real answer to what he calls the "tragedy of fetishism" and all its dilemmas: how can people so deeply enmeshed in fetishism liberate themselves from the system? Marx's answer is that through their own emancipatory praxis, people change society and change their own consciousness at the same time. It is only by their practical experience of struggle that people can liberate themselves of fetishism. This is also why the only true emancipation is self-emancipation and not liberation 'from above'. Any self-emancipatory action, individual or collective, however modest, may be a first step towards the 'expropriation of the expropriators'. But I don't believe that any "No", however barbaric, can be a 'driving force' as J.H. suggests on page 205: I don't think that suicide, going mad, terrorism and all sorts of anti-human responses to the system can be 'starting points' for emancipation. Just to give the obvious exemple: Ben Laden is not a starting point, it is a blind alley.

I like the conclusion of the book – without an end. We all are searching our way, no one can say he has found the true and only strategy. And we all have to learn from the living experience of struggles, like those of the Zapatistas.

* From the *New Politics* website:
  http://www.wpunj.edu/newpol/default.htm

First published by *Capital and Class*:
http://www.cseweb.org.uk

84

Phil Hearse
Take the power to change the world

16 October 2004

Written version of Hearse's speech in the debate on 'Strategies for Social Transformation', at the European Social Forum, October 16, 2004. The other speakers were John Holloway, Fausto Bertinotti and Hilary Wainwright.

Subcommandante Marcos focused this debate in the 1990s by his declaration that the Zapatistas refused, as a matter of principle, to fight for state power. I don't want to attack Marcos too much, because in my opinion the real start of the anti-globalisation movement and the fightback against neoliberalism was the Zapatista uprising on 1 January 1994. But Marcos and those who think like him are wrong to believe that anti-capitalist social transformation is possible without dealing with the question of state power, by simply turning your back on the state.

This can be seen by looking at some crucial contemporary social struggles. First, Argentina. In my opinion in the last four years the social and political struggle in Argentina has been the most advanced in the world. When the Argentinean economy collapsed in December 2001, a direct result of 'dollarisation' and extreme neo-liberal policies, the savings and livelihood of millions of working class and middle class Argentineans was expropriated. This led to a massive social explosion.

As a consequence a massive process of self-organisation developed, including the formation of neighbourhood and factory committees, the occupation of factories, which continued production under workers' self-management, the piqueteros movement, and many other forms of struggle. Self-organisation on a massive scale, while all the capitalist parties and leaders were completely discredited. But where is this movement today? It has largely disappeared or even been co-opted into government work projects at poverty wages.

Naomi Klein wrote a widely published article in which she said the decline of the mass movement was because of the sectarianism of the far-left organisations. She claims they brought their ideological arguments and petty squabbles into the movement, and as a consequence the masses became bored and frustrated and went home.

I don't discount the possibility that there is an element of truth on what she says about these organisations, but it is not the fundamental problem. The basic problem is that there was no big anti-capitalist party capable of uniting the movements and struggles in an overall project for taking the power. That's my criticism of the Argentinean left groups – that despite all the opportunities, they failed to create such a party on a united basis, despite having had more opportunities in the past 30 years than in most countries.

The decline of the Argentinean movement is a massive tragedy because for a time in that country there was a real vacuum at the top, and an anti-capitalist way out of the crisis was possible. Now we just have capitalist normalisation and the return of the corrupt and right-wing Peronists. As James Petras has put it, "The original strength of the popular uprising – its spontaneous, mass, autonomous character – became its strategic weakness, the absence of a national leadership capable of unifying the diverse forces behind a coherent program aimed at taking state power." (This article is available at www.rebelion.com)

The same problem is posed in a different context in Venezuela. In 2003 the London Observer newspaper published a very interesting article reporting from the massively self-organised barrios in Caracas. The reporter told of how the people were taking over the schools and utilities like water and electricity, organising literacy campaigns and so on. One militant told the reporter "We don't want a government like that of Hugo Chavez to represent us, we want to be the government." This article also told of some hostility to the Bolivarian circles among some barrio activists, accusing them of dragging politics into the struggles.

I sympathise with these anti-government and anti-state feelings, but ultimately they are a dead-end and a trap. Why is there this tremendous Bolivarian process, this enormous level of struggle against the right wing and the bourgeoisie, in Venezuela? *Because of the election of a left-wing government.* Where have all the resources come from for the literacy campaign, the pension and wage increases, the free children's breakfast programme? From the government, of course.

If you say we must turn your back on the state and power, then it becomes a matter of indifference, completely irrelevant, if Hugo Chavez is defeated in the right-wing referendum, because all that is about the state and doesn't concern us.

In reality, if Hugo Chavez had been defeated in the August 23 referendum it would have been a massive defeat for the Bolivarian revolutionary process – in fact it would have ended it in a carnival of reaction. Vast numbers of the working class and the poor understood this and did not turn their backs on Chavez and their revolution. They came down from the barrios in their millions to vote for Chavez and deal the hysterical bourgeoisie, the reactionary petty-bourgeoisie and US imperialism a fearful political blow.

Now I don't say that Chavez, a left-wing populist, is the final answer to socialist transformation in Venezuela. I say we defend him against the right wing. But to progress towards the victory of the Bolivarian revolution the Venezuelan masses need to create their own self-organised system of national administration. That's not turning your back on the state, that's creating a different kind of state and a different kind of power.

You can see the same thing in Mexico. The Zapatistas have created their own self-organised space in the highland villages of Chiapas, formally declaring their own independent municipalities in September 2003. All that is true. But it is the product of very particular circumstances, of geographical isolation and the fact that these communities are defended by the whole of Mexican civil society. For the moment, it is too politically dangerous for the Mexican bourgeoisie to launch any kind of all-out attack. In the future, this could easily change.

However, autonomy has not solved the problems of the Zapatista base communities. They are impoverished communities, and the people there share the same problems of health, of nutrition and of living standards of poor people in may other parts of Mexico. Because the Zapatista movement raises questions which cannot be solved simply at the level of their own communities, or even at the level of the whole of Chiapas. To bring the indigenous people of Chiapas out of poverty, you need social transformation at (at least) an all-Mexico level.

I will pose John Holloway a question. The Zapatistas have created their own liberated zone, through their own uprising. But suppose the same thing happened all across Mexico – the masses rose up and took control of their own workplaces and communities. Now, shouldn't these self-organised communities in Veracruz, in Monterrey, in Mexico City, in Guadalajara – shouldn't they talk to each other? Plan their futures together? Co-ordinate their economic plans in an overall plan of social development of Mexico? Elect recallable representatives to an all-Mexico assembly to decide these things? Co-ordinate their response to the massive counter-revolutionary wave which is sure to hit them from inside and outside the country?

Obviously they should. If they simply turn their back on the Mexican capitalist state without replacing it with something else, well the capitalist state will not turn its back on them. But if they do create their own national, self-governed co-ordination, than they will have created what is the slogan of the whole of the militant Mexican left – "Un gobierno obrera, campesino, indigena y popular" – a workers', peasant, indigenous and popular government. Not only that: they will have created an alternative form of power, an alternative form of state. Exactly what Marx called the 'Commune state'.

John Holloway rejects both any alternative form of state and any form of political party. In my opinion the refusal to form political parties of the left, and a refusal to fight for any alternative form of state power, are both disastrous choices.

Today in many parts of the world there is an enormous crisis of political representation of the working class and the oppressed, as a result of the old social democratic and Stalinist parties going off to the right. This threatens the presence of the working class in the national political arena, and far from being a positive thing, this has a negative impact not only on the national political discourse, but on the struggles and mass campaigns as well. To see this, look at the example of the Scottish Socialist Party (SSP).

The SSP now has six deputies in the Scottish parliament and a significant electoral impact (up to 10% of the vote). Is this a bad thing, a diversion? I don't think so. In fact the activity of the SSP deputies, who are always on the picket lines outside factories, who have led the campaign against racist immigrations laws and the Iraq war, and who are regularly being arrested protesting outside the Faslane nuclear submarine base, is a positive factor in the struggles, and not counterposed to it.

Equally the existence of Ridondazione Comunista in Italy or the United Left in Spain is, for the moment at least, a very positive factor for the struggle. I agree with Antonio Gramsci: the political party is the 'modern prince'. Social struggle always strives to find a political representation, and this we cannot turn our backs on. Today means not trying to find largely mythical autonomous spaces in which we can try to hide from the state, but building united left parties on an anti-capitalist basis to propel the struggle forward. Another world is possible, *but not without a revolution.*

M Junaid Alam
Taking power seriously –
a response to John Holloway

John Holloway, well-known left intellectual and author of the popular polemic *Change the World Without Taking Power: The Meaning of Revolution Today*, recently offered a concise presentation of his strategic vision on revolutionary change at ZNet. In his essay there, he strongly rejects the idea of approaching or seizing the state as an instrument for achieving social change, and encourages the notion of multiplying various kinds of incipient rebellions that bypass the state as the most fruitful path to human self-determination.

In advancing his thesis, however, Holloway fails to take stock of important current political developments or ground his definition of capitalism in a concrete context. As a result, he makes a number of simplistic assertions and leans on certain false dichotomies about the state and the process of revolutionary change. By examining these flaws, I think it is possible to show that Holloway's concept of "changing the world without taking power" is, unfortunately, trapped in a narrow framework where premises hang from a ceiling of intellectual defeatism and conclusions crash into walls of political paralysis.

Holloway's broadside against taking power is stern and unequivocal: he warns that "focus(ing) our struggle on the state" or "tak(ing) it as a principle point of reference" "leads us in the wrong direction." He writes, "The state...is a form of social relations...developed over several centuries for the purpose of maintaining or developing the rule of capital." Therefore, "we have to understand that the state pulls us in a certain direction." How? "It seeks to impose upon us a separation of our struggles from society"; it "separates leaders from the masses"; it "pulls us into a process of reconciliation with reality, and that reality is capitalism, a form of social organization that is based on exploitation and injustice, on killing and destruction." Worse, it "also draws us into a spatial definition of how we do things," one which not only "makes clear distinction between the state's territory and the world outside," but also "has no hope of matching the global movement of capital." These then are Holloway's most salient points against state-centered struggle.

The fundamental problem with all these concerns is that they could be raised anywhere. For instance, Holloway posits struggle within the state as a "reconciliation with reality," as capitulation, because after all the state represents the "reality of capitalism." But is the "reality of capitalism" not everywhere? Private institutions, organizations, cultural mores, and the entire general social milieu are all thoroughly penetrated and profoundly shaped by capitalism. Indeed, that is precisely why all these elements must be resisted and contested in the first place. What occurs vis-à-vis the state in particular, however, is not a "reconciliation" with the reality of capitalism, but a confrontation with the reality of capitalism by forces *opposed* to capitalism in its most important arena of control.

Turning to the issue of leaders becoming separated from masses, nothing about this process is exclusive to the state either. Leaders can betray, deceive, or abandon whoever they are tasked with representing in any social situation where money, power, and politics is involved – the workplace, the sports club, the university, the union, and so on. The difference is only that the stakes are higher when the state is involved. This cannot be invoked as an excuse to abandon social situations in general or the state in particular, since that would amount to total inaction. Leaders must be held accountable through concrete organizational mechanisms, and masses must themselves stay conscious and vigilant: it is this interplay which determines in the end how effectively and faithfully any leaders represent those who choose them.

The objection that taking on the state apparatus confines oneself to certain parameters of struggle – "spatial definitions" – could also be invoked in any other scenario. To struggle is necessarily to place oneself in the specific arena where struggle is being waged – preferably at its highest, sharpest level. This is true whether one is speaking of physical terrain on a military battlefield, ideological terrain on a political battlefield, or national terrain on a state-centered battlefield. One is, in fact, always "drawn" into "spatial definitions" no matter what one does. The question is only whether one chooses the space of concrete struggle, or the space of empty retreat.

On this score, to condemn state-centered struggle because it has "no hope" of combating "global capital" is to merely tinker with words, since capital is only global in the sense that it plants itself in every nation by negotiating access *through state permission*. Global capital is resisted partially when one state demands to set the terms of national development; it is resisted more forcefully when a bloc of states demand the same; and it is resisted *not at all* when the state has acquiesced to capital's demands – because revolutionaries there decided to let the state fall into right-wing hands by refusing to be "drawn into spatial definitions," or rather, by accepting the spatial definition of defeat.

Ultimately, Holloway's sweeping assertions about flaws in state-centered struggle are misleading for two reasons. One, the same kinds of flaws exist in any other sphere of struggle. Two, and most important, state-centered struggle does not *create* flaws in movements, but rather *reveals* them. For as we have seen, the only difference in regards to the state is one of degree: because the power of capitalism is so deeply entrenched within the state, the true strengths and limitations of any movement are exposed in confrontation with it. Avoiding confrontation may allow a movement to hide its weaknesses, and it may lead to some short-term self-glorification, but it will also avoid solving the actual problem. The viability of any revolutionary movement is determined by how effectively it is able to confront the system exactly in that arena where the system has been crafting *the injustices that gave rise to the movement in the first place*. It is not clear why Holloway believes the answer is to abandon the arena altogether, instead of working on new ways to address the flaws of the movement which are revealed within it.

What would be most instructive in examining Holloway's case for changing the world without taking power, however, is to look at a movement that has taken power and is carrying out change: the Bolivarian Revolution in Venezuela. Here is a living, breathing example of social struggle, where it is possible for us to examine in real terms and without theorizing what actually happens in a genuine revolutionary process.

What has the revolutionary government of Hugo Chavez Frias accomplished? It has undertaken a land reform program placing hundreds of thousands of hectares of idle land in the hands of small farmers and the landless poor; it has made education free for all from elementary through university level, offering students free daily meals; it has created special banks to assist women, small businesses, worker cooperatives, and farmers; it has locked into place the nationalization of the oil industry; it has organized vaccinations and community campaigns to increase literacy, training 1.3 million people to read; it has enlisted the previously unemployed to repair sanitation and transportation infrastructure; it has established 300 free health and dental clinics in slums where medical care has never been seen before;

it has introduced price controls on 160 basic foodstuffs and 60 essential household goods, subsidizing food markets in poor communities.

It is unfortunate – though perhaps not surprising, given the implications for his thesis – that Holloway fails to even mention this most remarkable development in his article. For what the Venezuelan example illustrates above all is that the anarchist notion of the state as intrinsically negative – a notion Holloway expresses most openly when he writes, "Betrayal is already given in the state as an organizational form" – is untenable as any sort of universally applicable position. Indeed, it would take a fanciful imagination to pretend that Chavez, who has played a decisive role in improving the lives of millions within his country, has "betrayed" the revolutionary process.

It follows from the reality in Venezuela that Holloway's previously-discussed reasons for abandoning state-centered struggle are not sustainable either. Chavez did not "reconcile" himself to capitalism, he used state power to help break capitalist political control and declare the path of revolution; he was not defeated by "spatial definitions," but seized upon the spatial definition of the historical narrative of Simon Bolivar to animate and excite the national imagination; he was not crushed by "the global movement of capital," but snatched it by the throat, prevented oil privatization, and pumped $3.7 billion dollars derived from state-controlled oil revenues into social investment in just one year. Thus we see that the conquest of state power was not only not a barrier, it was *an essential part* of carrying out and defending the concrete improvements made on the ground.

The Venezuelan example, then, deals a blow to the anarchist shibboleth of the state as inherently reactionary. But it would be a serious mistake to think that it vindicates the equally erroneous vangaurdist shibboleth that posits people as subjects to be trained by an enlightened state leadership. Caught between these false dichotomies of "good people/bad state" versus "bad people/good state", Holloway not only adopts the anarchist end of this view, but wrongly dismisses all state-centered struggle as lying on the vangaurdist end. He writes: "The state oriented-argument can be seen as a pivoted conception of the development of struggle", whereby, "First, we concentrate all our efforts on winning the state," and "then...we can think of revolutionizing society." This description, aside from being a caricature of the way most socialists conceive of revolutionary change, is very far off the mark in explaining what has happened in Venezuela.

For while it is undoubtedly true that holding state power has helped Chavez mount a strong defense of the revolutionary project, he did not simply do this overnight, nor did he do it by himself. The Chavez government would neither be in power nor have the political strength to carry out any of its policies even while in power had there not been an intense, dialectical process of engagement with the people who comprise the backbone of the revolution. Time and time again, it has been the active mobilization of the people from the slums – those who have felt that it is their government under attack – which has thwarted the right-wing forces of the oligarchy, media elite and embittered sections of the middle classes still aiming to unseat the revolution.

Through a constant process of support, feedback, initiative, pressure, frustration criticism, and, most importantly, mass demonstrations, it has been the masses who have propelled the revolution forward, strengthening and consolidating it every step of the way. In just a period of a few years, the revolution has fought and won a wave of battles: a short-lived right-wing coup, ratification of a new constitution, judiciary reform, two national legislative elections, two presidential elections, a business-led oil industry sabotage campaign, an attempted referendum recall, a viciously dishonest corporate-owned media – and, of course, the United States.

Throughout all this, the government, which certainly did not start out by declaring itself socialist, was forced to either start meeting the expectations of the people or risk finding its basis of support disappear. It had to answer concretely the demands and concerns of supporters like Juan Blanco, who complained shortly after the opposition launched its debilitating national strike in December 2002, "The assistance we get is very small; we do not even feel it. I ask, what is the goal of the revolution – where are we headed?" To which Chavez has now supplied the answer we are all familiar with: "I am convinced, and I think that this conviction will be for the rest of my life, that the path to a new, better and possible world, is not capitalism, the path is socialism."

It is unfortunate that Holloway, in accepting the framework of false dichotomies about state and people, necessarily rejects the state and the electoral arena as a site of social struggle. It robs him of the ability to see that the construction of socialism is a process and not one of absolute, fixed immovable forces; that in this process the state can be a vehicle for change precisely to the degree that the people are pushing for change through the state. The great strength in this approach, in the context of a revolutionary program, is that it constitutes an active, positive initiative in which concrete, visible gains can be made, defended and referenced. The poor can be fed, schools can be built, children can be taught, the sick can be treated – in the assets of the state lies the active, real basis for cultivating the soil from which the flowers of humanist values may blossom.

But by dint of his ideological disposition Holloway is forced to look to the negative – 'rebellions' and 'insubordinations,' the central focus of which is "people saying no to capitalism, no, we shall not live our lives according to the dictates of capitalism, we shall do what we consider necessary or desirable and not what capitalism tells us to do." He calls for "multiply(ing) and expand(ing) these refusals." The underlying problem with this approach is that saying no only goes so far no matter how many times one repeats it. It is intrinsically a negative demand and implies a program of only reflexive reaction, not positive action.

Moreover, it turns out that often times 'doing what we consider necessary' actually coincides with 'the dictates of capitalism' because capitalism is a totalizing force. Holloway, in describing capitalism as "not (in the first place) an economic system, but a system of command," proposes we break this control through refusal: "To refuse to obey is to break the command of capital." But this is misleading because the means of enforcing the 'system of command' is rooted in the 'economic system' itself. The state commands, coordinates, develops, defends, and appropriates a vast amount of capital, and, in so doing, *sets the basis* for its further ability to regulate a wide array of social relations and organizations upon which people depend in their everyday lives.

In this sense, then, capitalism is not so much 'a system of command" but a system of tenuous consent – people must work within the system in order to eat, to live, to buy things, and to maintain their position in society. Therefore to 'refuse to obey' in the immediate sense is not to 'break the command of capital' but rather to break one's connection to the social and support structure made possible by capital; it is to become isolated, atomized, individuated, and assigned to oblivion. This process is accelerated by the fact that, if a 'refusal' turns into more militant forms of insubordination with any sign of creating 'trouble,' the state unleashes its energies and either marginalizes and demoralizes the movement or crushes it ruthlessly.

The only way to change this situation is to translate the idea of resistance into positive action aimed at building an alternative society. Naturally, this requires an economic basis – a project which cannot be achieved by any kind of magic, by NGOs, by 'civil society,' or by any other scattered, isolated, nebulous group hovering and floating about on the margins. It can only be achieved by a broad democratic mass movement which understands, among other things, the necessity of controlling that hub which has been responsible for overseeing the theft of our labor and channeling the wealth we produce upwards and in ways designed to control and fragment us: the state.

The goal of this control should be twofold: to *remove* what is destructive and to *re-energize* what is productive for the ascending movement of human liberation. It is impossible to speculate in the abstract what in the state would warrant removal and what would warrant renewal; one might make broad references to decreasing armaments, eliminating advisory boards for corporations, reorienting research away from environmentally hazardous chemicals and toward cures for the ills those chemicals have caused, increasing funds for public education, transportation – and so on.

The guiding idea, however, should be to dethrone *power without principle* and coronate *principle without power*. That is to say, we must strive for the empowerment of our humanist principles as well as the disempowerment of unprincipled power. It is this dual process which will help break apart the old array of social relations and open up the path to genuine human development and solidarity among humankind.

Daniel Bensaid
The return of strategy

Daniel Bensaïd is a leading member of the Ligue Communiste Révolutionnaire (LCR) in France. This article was first published in the LCR's theoretical journal Critique Communiste, March 2006. It takes up issues arising in a discussion on revolutionary strategy in Critique Communiste and continued at a seminar in Paris in June. Other participants included Critique Communiste's editor Antoine Artous, LCR members Cedric Durand and Francis Sitel, and Alex Callinicos of the British SWP.[1] The issues involved ranged from the nature of socialist revolution today, to the attitude taken to non-revolutionary but anti-neoliberal forces in France. Explanatory notes and the translation are by permission of International Socialism: www.isj.org.uk

---

There has been an 'eclipse' in the debate about strategy since the beginning of the 1980s, in contrast with the discussions prompted by the experiences in the 1970s of Chile and Portugal (and then Nicaragua and Central America). The neoliberal offensive made the 1980s at best a decade of social resistance, characterised by a defensiveness in the class struggle, even in those cases when popular democratic pressure forced dictatorships to give way – notably in Latin America.

The withdrawal from politics found expression in what could be called a 'social illusion', by analogy with the 'political illusion' of those criticised by the young Marx for thinking 'political' emancipation through the achievement of civil rights was the last word in 'human emancipation'. There was an illusion about the self-sufficiency of social movements reflected in the experiences after Seattle (1999) and the first World Social Forum in Porto Alegre (2001).

Simplifying somewhat, I call this the 'utopian moment' of social movements, which took different forms: utopias based on the regulation of free markets; Keynesian utopias; and above all neo-libertarian utopias, in which the world can be changed without taking power or by making do with counter-powers (John Holloway, Toni Negri, Richard Day).

The upturn in social struggles turned into political or electoral victories in Latin America – Venezuela and Bolivia. But in Europe the struggles ended in defeat, except with the movement against the CPE attacks on the rights of young workers. The push towards privatisation, reforms in social protection and the dismantling of social rights could not be prevented. This lack of social victories has caused expectations to turn once more towards political (mostly electoral) solutions, as the Italian elections showed.[2]

This 'return of politics' has led to a revival in debates about strategy. Witness the polemics round the books of Holloway, Negri and Michael Albert, and the differing appraisals of the Venezuelan process and of Lula's administration in Brazil. There has been the shift in the Zapatistas' orientation with the sixth declaration of the Selva Lacandona and the 'other campaign' in Mexico. The discussions around the project for a new LCR manifesto or Alex Callinicos's Anticapitalist Manifesto[3] belong in the same context. We are coming to the end of the phase of the big refusal and of stoical resistance − Holloway's 'scream' in the face of "the mutilation of human lives by capitalism", slogans like "The world is not a commodity" or "Our world is not for sale". We need to be specific about what the 'possible' world is and, above all, to explore how to get there.

There is strategy and strategy

Notions of strategy and tactics are military terms that were imported into the workers' movement − above all from the writings of Clausewitz or of Delbrück. However, their meaning has varied greatly. At one time strategy was the art of winning a battle, with tactics being no more than troop manoeuvres. Since then there has been no halt to the expansion of the field of strategy over time and space, from dynastic wars to national wars, from total war to global war. So we can make a distinction today between global strategy operating on a world scale and 'limited strategy' concerned with the struggle for the conquest of power within a particular area. In some ways, the theory of permanent revolution sketched out a global strategy. The revolution starts from the national arena (in one country) to expand to the continental and world level; it takes a decisive step with the conquest of political power but is prolonged and deepened by 'a cultural revolution'. It thus combines act and process, event and history.

This dimension of global strategy is even more important today than it was in the first half of the 20th century, faced as we are with powerful states whose economic and military strategies are worldwide. The emergence of new strategic areas at the continental or world level shows this. The dialectic of the permanent revolution (as against the theory of socialism in one country), in other words the intertwining of national, continental and world levels, is tighter than ever. One can seize the levers of power in one country (like Venezuela or Bolivia), but the question of continental strategy (etc) immediately becomes a matter of domestic policy – as in the Latin American discussions over Alba versus Alca[A], a the relationship to Mercosur, to the Andes Pact. More prosaically, in Europe resistance to neoliberal counter-reforms can be reinforced by the balance of forces at the national level and by legislative gains. But a transitional approach to public services, taxation, social protection, ecology has to be pitched at the European level from the outset.[4]

Strategic hypotheses

I confine myself here to the question of what I have called 'the limited strategy' – the struggle for the conquest of political power at the national level. The framework of globalisation can weaken national states and some transfers of sovereignty take place. But the national rung, which structures class relationships and attaches a territory to a state, remains the decisive rung in the sliding scale of strategic spaces.

Let us straightaway put aside the criticisms from those like John Holloway and Cédric Durand[5] that ascribe to us a 'stagist' vision of the revolutionary process, according to which we would make the seizure of power the 'absolute precondition' for any social transformation. The argument is either a caricature or it stems from ignorance. Vaulting from a standing start is not something we have ever been keen on.

The concepts of the united front, of transitional demands and of the workers' government – defended not just by Trotsky but by Thalheimer, Radek and Clara Zetkin[6] – have a precise aim. This is to link the event to its preparatory conditions, revolution to reforms, the goal to the movement. The Gramscian notions of hegemony and 'war of position' operate along the same lines.[7] The opposition between the East (where power would be easier to conquer but more difficult to maintain) and the West arises from the same concern.[8] We have never been admirers of the theory of the mere collapse of the system.[9]

We have insisted on the role of the 'subjective factor' as against both the spontaneist view of the revolutionary process and the structuralist immobilism of the 1960s. Our insistence is not on a 'model' but on what we have called 'strategic hypotheses'.[10] Models are something to be copied; they are instructions for use. A hypothesis is a guide to action that starts from past experience but is open and can be modified in the light of new experience or unexpected circumstances. Our concern therefore is not to speculate but to see what we can take from past experience, the only material at our disposal. But we always have to recognise that it is necessarily poorer than the present and the future if revolutionaries are to avoid the risk of doing what the generals are said to do – always fight the last war.

Our starting point lies in the great revolutionary experiences of the 20th century – the Russian Revolution, the Chinese Revolution, the German Revolution, the popular fronts, the Spanish Civil War, the Vietnamese war of liberation, May 1968, Portugal, Chile. We have used them to distinguish between two major hypotheses, or scenarios: that of the insurrectional general strike and that of the extended popular war. They encapsulate two types of crisis, two forms of dual power, two ways of resolving the crisis.

As far as the insurrectional general strike is concerned, dual power takes a mainly urban form, of the Commune variety – not just the Paris Commune, but the Petrograd Soviet, the insurrections in Hamburg in 1923, Canton in 1927, Barcelona in 1936. Dual power cannot last long in a concentrated area. Confrontation therefore leads to a rapid resolution, although this may in turn lead to a prolonged confrontation: civil war in Russia, the liberation war in Vietnam after the 1945 insurrection. In this scenario the task of demoralising the army and organising the soldiers plays an important part. Among the more recent and meaningful experiences in this respect were the soldiers' committees in France, the SUV 'Soldiers united will win' movement in Portugal in 1995, and the conspiratorial work of the MIR[B] in the Chilean army in 1972-73.

In the case of the extended popular war strategy, the issue is one of territorial dual power through liberated and self-administered zones, which can last much longer. Mao understood the conditions for this as early as his 1927 pamphlet Why is it that Red Political Power can Exist in China? and the experience of the Yenan Republic[C] shows how it operates.

According to the insurrectionary general strike scenario, the organs of alternative power are socially determined by urban conditions; according to the extended popular war scenario, they are centralised in the (predominantly peasant) 'people's army'.

There are a whole range of variants and intermediary combinations between these two hypotheses in their ideal form. So the Cuban Revolution made the guerrilla foco ('focus') the link between the kernel of the rebel army and attempts to organise and call urban general strikes in Havana and Santiago.[11] The relationship between the two was problematic, as shown in the correspondence of Frank País[D], Daniel Ramos Latour and Che himself about the tensions between 'the sierra' and 'the plain'. Retrospectively, the official narrative privileged the heroic epic of the Granma[E] and its survivors. This contributed to bolstering the legitimacy of that element in the 26 July Movement and of the ruling Castro group, but was detrimental to a more complex understanding of the process.

This simplified version of history was set up as a model for rural guerrilla war and inspired the experiences of the 1960s in Peru, Venezuela, Nicaragua, Colombia, Bolivia. The deaths of De La Puente and Lobatòn in Peru (1965), Camillo Torres in Colombia (1966), Yon Sosa and Lucio Cabañas in Mexico, Carlos Marighela and Lamarca in Brazil, the tragic expedition of Che to Bolivia, the near annihilation of the Sandinistas in 1963 and 1969, the disaster of Teoponte in Bolivia in 1970, mark the end of that cycle.

The strategic hypothesis of the Argentinean PRT[F] and the MIR in Chile made greater use, at the beginning of the 1970s, of the Vietnamese example of extended popular war (and, in the PRT's case, of a mythic version of the Algerian war of liberation). The history of the Sandinista front up to its victory over the Somoza dictatorship in 1979 shows a mixture of different outlooks. The Prolonged People's War tendency of Tomàs Borge stressed the development of a guerrilla presence in the mountains and the need for a long period of gradually accumulating forces. The Proletariat Tendency of Jaime Wheelock insisted on the social effects of capitalist development in Nicaragua and on the strengthening of the working class while retaining the perspective of a prolonged accumulation of forces with a view to an 'insurrectional moment'. The 'Tercerista' Tendency of the Ortega brothers was a synthesis of the other two tendencies which allowed for coordination between the southern front and the uprising in Managua.

Looking back, Humberto Ortega summed up the differences thus:

"The politics which consists of not intervening in events, of accumulating forces from cold, is what I call the politics of passive accumulation of forces. This passivity was evident at the level of alliances. There was also passivity in the fact that we thought we could accumulate arms, organise ourselves, bring human resources together without fighting the enemy, without having the masses participate."[12]

He recognised that circumstances shook their various plans up:

"We called for the insurrection. The pace of events quickened, objective conditions did not allow us greater preparation. In reality, we could not say no to the insurrection − such was the breadth of the mass movement that the vanguard was incapable of directing it. We could not oppose this torrent. All we could do was to put ourselves at its head in the hope of more or less leading it and giving it a sense of direction."

He concluded, "Our insurrectional strategy always gravitated around the masses and not around some military plan. This must be clear." In reality, having a strategic option implies a sequencing of political priorities, of when to intervene, of what slogans to raise. It also determines the politics of alliances.

Mario Payeras's narrative of the Guatemala process[13] illustrates a return from the forest to the town and a change in relationships between the military and the political, the countryside and the town, and Régis Debray's 1974 A Critique of Arms (or self-criticism) also provides an account of the start of this evolution in the 1960s. There were the disastrous adventures of the Red Army Fraction in Germany, of the Weathermen[G] in the US (to say nothing of the ephemeral tragi-comedy of the Gauche prolétarienne[H] in France and the theses of July/Geismar[I] in their unforgettable Vers la Guerre Civile ('Towards Civil War') of 1969. All these and other attempts to translate the experience of rural guerrilla war into 'urban guerrilla' war came to a close in the 1970s. The only instances of armed movements to have lasted successfully were those whose organisations had their social base in struggles against national oppression (Ireland, the Basque Country).[14]

These strategic hypotheses and experiences were not simply reducible to militarism. They set political tasks in order. Thus the PRT's conception of the Argentinean Revolution as a national war of liberation meant privileging the construction of an army (the ERP) at the cost of self-organisation in workplaces and neighbourhoods. Similarly, the MIR's orientation of putting the stress, under Popular Unity, on accumulating forces (and rural bases) led to its downplaying the threat of a coup d'état and above all underestimating its long term consequences. Yet as MIR's general secretary Miguel Enriquez clearly perceived, following the failure of the first, abortive, coup of 29 June there was a brief moment favourable to the creation of a combat government which could have prepared for a trial of strength.

The Sandinista victory in 1979 no doubt marked a new turn. That at least is the view of Mario Payeras who stressed that in Guatemala (as in El

Salvador) revolutionary movements were not confronted by clapped out puppet dictatorships but by Israeli, Taiwanese and US 'advisers' in 'low intensity' and 'counter-revolutionary' wars. This increasing asymmetry has since gone global with the new strategic doctrines of the Pentagon and the declaration of 'unlimited' war against 'terrorism'.

This is one reason (in addition to the tragic hyperviolence of the Cambodian experience, the bureaucratic counter-revolution in the USSR, and the Cultural Revolution in China) why the question of revolutionary violence has become a thorny, even taboo, subject, whereas in the past the epic sagas of the Granma and of Che, or the writings of Fanon, Giap or Cabral made violence appear innocent or liberatory. What we see is a groping towards some asymmetrical strategy of the weak and the strong, an attempt to synthesise Lenin and Gandhi[15] or orient towards non-violence.[16] Yet the world has not become less violent since the fall of the Berlin Wall. It would be rash and otherworldly to bet on there being a 'peaceful way'. Nothing from the century of extremes ratifies this scenario.

The hypothesis of the insurrectional general strike

The guideline for our strategic hypothesis in the 1970s was the insurrectional general strike, which, for the most part, bore no resemblance to the variants of acclimatised Maoism and its imaginary interpretations of the Cultural Revolution. It is this hypothesis of which we are now the 'orphans', according to Antoine Artous[J]. What might have had a certain 'functionality' yesterday is lost today. He does not deny, however, the continuing relevance of notions of revolutionary crisis and dual power. The hypothesis needs, he insists, serious reformulation – one that avoids wallowing in the term 'rupture' and in verbal trickery. Two points crystallise his concern.

On the one hand, Antoine insists that dual power cannot be totally situated outside existing institutions and be made suddenly to spring from nothing in the form of a pyramid of soviets or councils. We may once upon a time have surrendered to this oversimplified vision of real revolutionary processes that we used to pore over in political study groups. But I doubt it. Be that as it may, other texts[17] swiftly corrected whatever vision we may have had. We may even, at the time, have been disturbed or shocked by Ernest Mandel coming round to the idea of 'mixed democracy'[K] after he had re-assessed the relationship between the soviets and the Constituent Assembly in Russia. Yet clearly one cannot imagine a revolutionary process other than as a transfer of legitimacy which gives preponderance to 'socialism from below' but which interacts with forms of representation, particularly in countries with parliamentary traditions going back over more than a century, and where the principle of universal suffrage is firmly established.

In practice, our ideas have evolved – as they did, for example, during the Nicaraguan Revolution. In the context of a civil war and a state of siege, organising 'free' elections in 1989 was open to question but we did not challenge the principle. Rather we criticised the Sandinistas for suppressing the 'council of state'[L], which might have constituted a sort of second social chamber and have been a pole of alternative legitimacy to the elected parliament. Similarly, though on a more modest scale, the example of the dialectic in Porto Alegre between the municipal institution (elected by universal suffrage) and participatory committees over the budget is worth consideration.

The problem we face is not in reality that of the relationship between territorial democracy and workplace democracy (the Paris Commune, the soviets and the Setubal popular assembly of Portugal in 1975 were territorial structures), nor even that of the relationship between direct and representative democracy (all democracy is partially representative). The real problem is how the general will is formed.

Most criticism of soviet-style democracy by the Eurocommunists[M] or by Norberto Bobbio[N] is targeted at its tendency to corporatism: a sum (or pyramid) of particular interests (parochial, workplace, office), linked by a system of mandating, could not allow for the creation of the general will. Democratic subsidiarity has its drawbacks too. If the inhabitants of a valley are opposed to a road passing through it or if a town is against having a waste collection centre (in order to palm both off on their neighbours), then there really has to be some form of centralised arbitration.[18] In our debates with the Eurocommunists we insisted on the necessary mediation (and plurality) of parties so that a synthesis of propositions could emerge and a general will arise out of particular viewpoints. Our programmatic documents have increasingly incorporated the general hypothesis of a dual chamber. But we have not ventured into speculation about institutional nuts and bolts – the practical details remain open to experience.

Antoine Artous's second concern, notably in his criticism of Alex Callinicos, bears on the assertion that Alex's transitional approach halts at the threshold of the question of power. This would be left to be resolved by some unconvincing deus ex machina,[O] supposedly by a spontaneous tidal wave of the masses and a generalised outburst of soviet democracy. Though defence of civil liberties figures prominently in Alex's programme, he would appear to make no demands of an institutional nature (for example, the demand for proportional representation, a constituent assembly or single chamber, or radical democratisation). Cédric Durand, on the other hand, would seem to conceive of institutions as mere intermediaries for autonomous protest strategies. This, in practice, might boil down to a compromise between 'below' and 'above' – in other words, crude lobbying by the former of the latter, which is left intact.

In reality all sides in the controversy agree on the fundamental points inspired by The Coming Catastrophe (Lenin's pamphlet of the summer of 1917) and the Transitional Programme of the Fourth International (inspired by Trotsky in 1937): the need for transitional demands, the politics of alliances (the united front),[19] the logic of hegemony and on the dialectic (not antinomy) between reform and revolution. We are therefore against the idea of separating an ('anti-neoliberal') minimum programme and an (anti-capitalist) 'maximum' programme. We remain convinced that a consistent anti-neoliberalism leads to anti-capitalism and that the two are interlinked by the dynamic of struggle.

We can argue about exactly how the balance of forces and existing levels of consciousness should structure transitional demands. Agreement is easy, however, on targeting the privatisation of the means of production, communication and exchange – whether in relation to public sector education, humanity's common goods or the increasingly important question of the socialisation of knowledge (as opposed to intellectual private property). Similarly, we can easily agree on exploring ways to socialise wages through systems of social protection as a step towards the withering away of the wages system altogether. Finally, in opposition to the generalisation of the market we open up the possibilities of extending the free provision of, not merely services, but basic items of consumption (thus of 'de-marketisation').

The tricky question about the issue of transition is that of the 'workers' government'. The difficulty is not new. The debates at the time of the fifth congress of the Communist International (1924) on the record of the German Revolution and the Social Democrat-Communist governments of Saxony and Thuringia in the late summer of 1923 before show this. They reveal the unresolved ambiguity of the formulae that came out of the early congresses of the Communist International and the range of interpretations which they could give rise to in practice. Treint[P] underlined in his report that "the dictatorship of the proletariat does not fall from the sky; it must have a beginning and the workers' government is synonymous with the start of the dictatorship of the proletariat." Nevertheless he denounced the 'Saxonisation' of the united front: "The entry of the communists into a coalition government with bourgeois pacifists to prevent an intervention against the revolution was not wrong in theory" but governments of the Labour Party or Left Bloc type cause "bourgeois democracy to find an echo within our own parties".

The Czechoslovak Smeral declared in the debate on the activity of the International: 'As far as the theses of our congress in February 1923 on the workers' government are concerned, we were all convinced when we drew them up that they were in line with the decisions of the fourth congress. They were adopted unanimously." But "what are the masses thinking about when they speak of a workers' government?" "In England, they think of the Labour Party, in Germany and in other countries where capitalism is decomposing, the united front means that the communists and social democrats, instead of fighting one another when the strike breaks out, are marching shoulder to shoulder. For the masses the workers' government has the same meaning and when we use this formula they imagine a united government of all the workers' parties." And Smeral continued: "What deep lesson does the Saxon experiment teach us? Above all, this: that one cannot vault from a standing start – a run-up is needed."

Ruth Fischer's[Q] answer was that as a coalition of workers' parties the workers' government would mean "the liquidation of our party". In her report on the failure of the German Revolution Clara Zetkin argued:

"As far as the workers' and peasants' government is concerned I cannot accept Zinoviev's declaration that it is simply a pseudonym, a synonym or god knows what homonym, for the dictatorship of the proletariat. That may be correct for Russia but it is not the same for countries where capitalism is flourishing. There the workers' and peasants' government is the political expression of a situation in which the bourgeoisie can no longer maintain itself in power but where the proletariat is not yet in a position to impose its dictatorship."

In fact, what Zinoviev defined as the 'elementary objective of the workers' government' was the arming of the proletariat, workers' control over production, a tax revolution…

One could go on and quote other contributions. The resulting impression would be of enormous confusion. This expresses a real contradiction and an inability to solve the problem, even though it was raised in a revolutionary or pre-revolutionary situation.

It would be irresponsible to provide a solution that is universally valid; nevertheless, three criteria can be variously combined for assessing participation in a government coalition with a transition perspective:

a) The question of participation arises in a situation of crisis or at least of a significant upsurge in social mobilisation, and not from a vacuum;

b) The government in question is committed to initiating a dynamic of rupture with the established order. For example – and more modestly than the arming of the workers demanded by Zinoviev – radical agrarian reform, 'despotic incursions' into the domain of private property, the abolition of tax privileges, a break with institutions like those of the Fifth Republic in France, European treaties, military pacts, etc;

c) Finally, the balance of forces allows revolutionaries to ensure that even if they cannot guarantee that the non-revolutionaries in the government keep to their commitments, they have to pay a high price for failure to do so.

In this light participation in the Lula government in Brazil[R] appears to have been mistaken:

a) For ten years or so, with the exception of the landless movement, the mass movement has been on the retreat.

b) the colour of Lula's social-neoliberal politics was clearly shown in his electoral campaign and in his Letter to the Brazilians (promising to keep to the previous government's financial commitments). The financing of his agrarian reform and 'zero-hunger' programme was mortgaged in advance

c) Finally, the social balance of forces within both the party and the government was such that to be a half-minister in agricultures was not to support the government "like a rope supports a hanged man" but rather like a hair that could not. That said, and taking into account the history of the country, its social structure and the formation of the PT, we chose not to make this a matter of principle (though we expressed our reservations orally to the comrades about participation and alerted them to the dangers). We preferred to go along with the experiment so as to draw up the balance sheet alongside the comrades, rather than give lessons 'from a distance'[S].[20]

About the dictatorship of the proletariat

The question of the workers' government has inevitably brought us back to the question of the dictatorship of the proletariat. An LCR conference decided by a majority of more than two thirds to remove mention of it from its statutes. That was fair enough. Today the term dictatorship more readily invokes the military or bureaucratic dictatorships of the 20th century than the venerable Roman institution of temporary emergency powers duly mandated by the Senate. Since Marx saw the Paris Commune as 'the political form at last discovered' of this dictatorship of the proletariat, we would be better off understood as invoking the Commune, the soviets, councils or self-management, rather than hanging on to a verbal fetish which history has rendered a source of confusion.

For all that we haven't done with the question raised by Marx's formula and the importance he gave it in his celebrated letter to Kugelman. Generally speaking, the 'dictatorship of the proletariat' tends to carry the image of an authoritarian regime and to be seen as a synonym for bureaucratic dictatorships. But for Marx it was the democratic solution to an old problem – the exercise for the first time by the (proletarian) majority of emergency power, which till then had been the preserve of a virtuous elite as with the Committee of Public Safety of the French Revolution, even if the committee in question emanated from the Convention and could be recalled by it. The term 'dictatorship' in Marx's time was often counterposed to 'tyranny', which was used to express despotism.

The notion of the dictatorship of the proletariat also had a strategic significance, one often raised in the debates of the 1970s upon its abandonment by the majority of (Euro)communist parties. Marx clearly grasped that the new legal power, as an expression of a new social relationship, could not be born if the old one remained: between two social legitimacies, 'between two equal rights, it is force that decides'. Revolution implies therefore a transition enforced by a state of emergency. Carl Schmitt[T], who was an attentive reader of the polemic between Lenin and Kautsky, understood perfectly what was at issue when he distinguished between the 'chief constable dictatorship', whose function in a state of crisis is to preserve the established order, and the 'sovereign dictatorship', which inaugurates a new order by virtue of a constitutive power.[21] If this strategic perspective, whatever name we give it, remains valid then there necessarily follows a series of consequences about how power is organised, about legitimacy, about how parties function, etc.

The actuality or otherwise of a strategic approach

The notion of 'the actuality of revolution'[U] has a double meaning: a broad sense ('the epoch of wars and revolution') and an immediate or conjectural sense. In the defensive situation the social movement finds itself in, having

108

been thrown back for more than 20 years in Europe, no one will claim that revolution has an actuality in an immediate sense. On the other hand, it would be a risky and not a minor matter to eliminate it from the horizon of our epoch. Perhaps Francis Sitel intended to use this distinction in his contribution to the debate. If he wants to avoid "a wild-eyed vision of the actual balance of forces" as 'a current perspective' and prefers instead a "perspective for action which informs present struggles about the necessary outcomes of these same struggles", then there is not much to quarrel about. But more debatable is the idea according to which we could maintain the objective of conquering power "as a sign of radicalism but admit that its realisation is currently beyond our horizon".

For him the question of government is not linked to the question of power, but to 'a more modest demand', that of 'protection' against the neoliberal offensive. The debate about the conditions for participation in government does not go "through the monumental gate of strategic reflection", but "through the narrow gate of broad parties". Our fear here is that it may no longer be the need for a programme (or strategy) which dictates the construction of the party but the size of an algebraically broad party which determines what is seen as the best party policy. The issue of government would then be scaled down as a strategic question and recast as a mere 'question of orientation' (which, to some extent, is what we did with Brazil). But a 'question of orientation' is not disconnected from the strategic perspective unless we fall into the classic dissociation between minimum and maximum programme. And, if 'broad' is necessarily more generous and open than narrow and closed, there are different degrees of broadness: the Brazilian PT, the Linkspartei in Germany, the ODP in Turkey, the Left Bloc in Portugal, Rifondazione Comunista, are not of the same nature.

"The most erudite developments in matters of revolutionary strategy appear quite airy fairy," Francis Sitel concludes, "compared with the question of how to act in the here and now." Certainly, this worthy pragmatic maxim could have been uttered in 1905, in February 1917, in May 1936, in February 1968, thus reducing the sense of the possible to one of prosaic realism.

Francis Sitel's diagnosis, and his programmatic adjustment to this side of the horizon, is not without practical implications. Once our perspective is no longer limited to seizing power but is inscribed in a longer process of 'subverting power', we would have to recognise that "the traditional[22] party which concentrates on the conquest of power is led to adapt to the state itself" and consequently "to transmit within itself mechanisms of domination which undermine the very dynamic of emancipation". A new dialectic has therefore to be invented between the political and the social. Certainly; this is the practical and theoretical task we set ourselves, when we reject 'the political illusion' as much as 'the social illusion', or draw principled conclusions from past negative experiences (about the independence of social organisations towards the state and parties, about political pluralism, about democracy within parties).

But the problem does not lie in the way a party 'adapted to the state' transmits the state's mechanisms of domination so much as in the deeper and commoner phenomenon of bureaucratisation, rooted in the division of labour. Bureaucratisation is inherent in modern societies: it affects trade union and associative organisations as a whole. In fact, party democracy (as opposed to the media-driven, plebiscitary democracy of so called 'public opinion') would be, if not an absolute remedy, at least one of the antidotes to the professionalisation of power and the 'democracy of the market'. This is too easily forgotten by those who see in democratic centralism only a mask for bureaucratic centralism. Yet some degree of centralisation is the very condition for democracy, not its negation.

The stress on the adaptation of the party to the state finds an echo in the isomorphism (picked up by Boltanski and Chiapello in The New Spirit of Capitalism) between the structure of capital itself and the structures of the workers' movement, which are subordinate to it. This question is a crucial one and cannot be evaded or resolved easily: the wage struggle and the right to a job (sometimes called the 'right to work') is indeed a struggle that is subordinate to (isomorphic with) the capital/labour relationship. Behind that is the whole problem of alienation, fetishism and reification. But to believe that 'fluid' forms – organising in networks and the logic of affinity groups (as opposed to the logic of hegemony) – escape this subordination is a grotesque illusion. Such forms are perfectly isomorphic with the modern organisation of computerised capital, flexible working, the 'liquid society', etc. That does not mean that the old forms of subordination were better or preferable to the emergent forms – only that there is no royal road of networking to lead us out of the vicious circle of exploitation and domination.

On the 'broad party'

Francis Sitel is fearful that talking of 'the eclipse' or 'the return of strategic reason' means simply bracketing things off, returning to the same old themes or taking up the question in the terms posed by the Third International. He insists on the need for 'fundamental revisions', for reinvention, for 'constructing something new', as fitting the requirements of the workers' movement. Of course. But we are not speaking of a blank screen. The rhetoric of novelty is no guarantee against falling back into the oldest, and most hackneyed, ways of thinking. Some new ways of thinking (about ecology, feminism, war and rights) are genuine. But many of the 'novelties' our epoch indulges in are no more than fashionable effects (feeding like any fashion on quotations from the past), which recycle old utopian themes from the 19th century and the workers' movement in its infancy.

Having rightly recalled that reforms and revolution form a dialectical couple in our tradition and not an opposition of mutually exclusive terms, Francis Sitel hazards the prediction that a "broad party will be defined as a party of reforms". That's as maybe. But it's an idea that is speculative and sets up a norm in advance. And that certainly is not our problem.

We don't have to put the cart before the horse and invent among ourselves a minimum programme (of reforms) for a hypothetical 'broad party'. We have to define our project and our programme. It is from that starting point that, in concrete situations and with tangible allies, we shall weigh up what compromises are possible, even if it means accepting some loss in clarity, in exchange for greater social spread, experience and dynamism. This is not new. We participated in the creation of the PT. Our comrades are active as a current in Rifondazione. They play a decisive part in the Left Bloc in Portugal. But these are all specific configurations and should not be brought together under some all-inclusive category of 'broad party'.

The structural situation in which we find ourselves certainly opens up a space to the left of the major traditional formations of the workers' movement (social democrats, Stalinists, populists). There are many reasons for this. The neoliberal counter-reform, the privatisation of the public arena, the dismantling of the welfare state, the market society, have sawn off the branch on which sat social democracy – and populist adminstrations in certain Latin American countries. The communist parties in Europe have suffered the after-effect of the implosion of the USSR at the same time as the erosion of the social bases they acquired in the pre-war years and the period of liberation from the Nazis, without gaining new roots. There really does exist what we often call a radical 'space', which has found diverse expression in the emergence of new social movements and electoral formations. This is the present day basis for reconstruction and regroupment.

But this 'space' is not homogenous and empty so that all we have to do is fill it. It is a highly unstable force field, as shown spectacularly by the conversion in less than three years of Rifondazione from lyrical movementism, at the time of Genoa and Florence,23 to government coalition with Romano Prodi. This instability stems from the fact that the social mobilisations have suffered more defeats than they have won victories and that their link to the transformation of the political landscape remains overstretched. In the absence of meaningful social victories, the hope of the 'lesser evil' ('anything but Berlusconi – or Sarkozy, or Le Pen!') moves, for lack of real change, to the electoral terrain where the weight of institutional logic remains decisive (in France, that of plebiscitary presidentialism and a particularly anti-democratic electoral system). That's why the symmetry of the happy medium, between an opportunist and a conservative danger is a false perspective: they don't carry the same weight. We must know how to dare to take risky decisions (the most extreme example being that of the October insurrection) – but we must also know how to weigh up the risk and calculate the chances if we are to avoid pure adventurism. As the great dialectician Pascal said, we are already committed – we must wager. Yet racegoers know that a bet of two to one is small time, and that a bet of a thousand to one, though it may hit the jackpot, is a desperate throw. The margin is between the two. Daring too has its reasons.

The evolution from right to left of currents like Rifondazione or the Linkspartei remains fragile (even reversible) for the very reason that the effects of social struggle on the field of political representation remain limited. It depends in part on the presence and weight within them of revolutionary organisations or tendencies.

There are very general common factors. But over and beyond these, conditions vary enormously, depending on the specific history of the workers' movement (for instance, whether social democracy is totally hegemonic or whether there subsist important communist parties). It also depends on the balance of forces within the left. Apparatuses are determined not only by ideology, but by social logics. They cannot be shifted by whispering in the ears of their leaders, but only by modifying the real balance of forces.

The perspective of a 'new force' remains an algebraic formula for now (this was true for us before 1989-91 and is even truer since). Translating it into practice cannot be mechanically deduced from formulae as vague and general as 'the broad party' or 'regroupment'. We are only at the start of a process of reconstruction. What counts in the approach to this is our programmatic compass and strategic aim. This is one condition that will allow us to discover the organisational mediations we need and to take calculated risks. That way we avoid throwing ourselves headlong into some impatient adventure and dissolving ourselves into the first ephemeral combination that comes along. Organisational formulae are in reality very variable, depending on whether at issue is a new mass party (like the PT in Brazil in the 1980s, though this is an unlikely pattern in Europe), minority splits from a hegemonic social democracy, or yet again parties that we might previously have termed centrist (Rifondazione five years ago), or a coalition of revolutionary currents (as in Portugal). This last hypothesis remains, however, the most likely for countries such as France, where there is a long tradition of organisations like the CP or the far left and where, without a really powerful social movement, for them simply to merge in the short or medium term is difficult to imagine.

But, in every case, reference to a common programmatic background, far from being something that obstructs future reconstruction, is on the contrary its precondition. Strategic and tactical questions can then be prioritised so that we are not torn apart because of this or that electoral outcome. We can distinguish the political base on which organising open theoretical debate makes sense. We can assess which compromises allow us to forge ahead and which pull us back. We can adjust to forms of organisational existence (whether to be a tendency in a shared party, part of a front, etc.), depending on our allies and how their dynamic fluctuates (from right to left or left to right).

Explanatory notes

A   Alba – the Bolivarian Alternative for Latin America and the Caribbean, proposed by Chavez. Alca – the Free Trade Area of the Americas, proposed by the US.

B   MIR – Chilean Movement of the Revolutionary Left.

C   The remote region of China run by the Chinese Communists from the mid-1930s to their taking of Beijing in 1949.

D   The leader of the urban resistance in Cuba, killed in 1958 shortly before the victory of the revolution.

E   The boat from which the group of guerrillas led by Castro landed in Cuba at the end of 1956.

F   PRT – Revolutionary Workers Party, an Argentinian section of the Fourth International with a guerrilla group, the ERP.

G   A guerrilla group formed from a split in Students for a Democratic Society, led by Bernadine Dohn and Mark Rudd.

H   A French Maoist organisation formed in 1969.

I   Serge July was editor of the daily Liberation from 1974 to 2006, steering it from Maoism to the neoliberal 'centre-left'; Alain Geismar, secretary of the lecturers' SNE-Sup union during the events of May 1968, then a Maoist, now Inspector General of Education.

J   Antoine Artous – editor of the LCR's theoretical journal Critique Communiste. Bensaïd is referring to Artous's article in that journal, translated as 'The LCR and the Left: Some Strategic Questions' in the International Socialist Tendency's International Discussion Bulletin 7 (January 2006), www.istendency.net

K   ie of a combination of parliament and workers' councils.

L   A body of around 50 people nominated from the political parties, the Sandinista defence committees, the unions, professional associations and private enterprise organisations.

M   Communists who broke with Stalinism in the late '60s and '70s to embrace left wing parliamentarianism.

N   Norberto Bobbio – a left of centre Italian political philosopher.

O   Latin phrase – 'A god from a machine', ie sudden emergence of a solution from nowhere.

P   Albert Treint – leader of the pro-Zinoviev wing of the French Communist Party in the mid-1920s.

Q   Ruth Fischer – leader of the ultra-left in the German Communist Party in the early and mid-1920s. She later became a fervent cold warrior.

R   By members of the DS current which is part of the Fourth International.

S   The position taken by a leading member of DS.

T   Right wing German legal theorist of the inter-war years, joined Nazi Party.

U   Term used by the Hungarian Marxist philosopher Georg Lukács in 1922.

Notes

1   The contributions are available on the website of the ESSF (Europe solidaire sans frontières). Texts by Artous and Alex Callinicos are translated in the International Discussion Bulletin of the International Socialist Tendency at www.istendency.net

2   This was Stathis Kouvelakis's emphasis in 'The Triumph of the Political', International Socialism 108 (Autumn 2005).

3   Alex Callinicos, An Anti-Capitalist Manifesto (Cambridge, 2003).

4   I shall go no further on this aspect of the question. It is simply a reminder (see in this respect the theses proposed in the debate organised by Das Argument).

5   Durand appears to attribute to us a 'stagist view of social change' and 'a temporality of political action centred exclusively on the preparation of the revolution as a decisive moment' (to which he opposes 'an altermondialist and Zapatista historical time' ??!!), see Critique Communiste 179. For a detailed critique of John Holloway's approach, see the detailed critique in Daniel Bensaïd, Un monde à changer (Paris, Textuel 2006); Planète altermondialiste (Textuel, 2006), and in articles in Contretemps.

6   In the debate about the programme in the Communist International up till its sixth congress.

7   See Perry Anderson, 'The Antinomies of Gramsci', New Left Review 100, 1977.

8   See the debates around the report on the German Revolution at the fifth congress of the Communist International.

9   See Giacomo Marramao, Il Politico e le trasformazioni, and the pamphlet Stratégies et partis.

10 As Antoine Artous reminds us in his article in Critique Communiste.

11 Despite the simplified myth of the foco, notably in Regis Debray, Revolution in the Revolution (London, 1967).

12 'The strategy for victory', interview by Marta Harnecker. Asked about the date on which the insurrection was called, Ortega replied: 'Because a whole series of more and more favourable objective conditions arose: the economic crisis, the currency devaluation, the political crisis. And because after the September events we realised that it was necessary to combine simultaneously and within the same strategic space the rising of the masses at a national level, the offensive of the military forces at the front and the national strike in which the employers were involved or in practice acquiesced. If we had not combined these three strategic factors simultaneously and in the same strategic space, victory would not have been possible. On several occasions there had been a call for a national strike, but it had not been combined with the mass offensive. The masses had already risen, but the rising had not been combined with strike action and took place at a time when the military capacity of the vanguard was too weak. And

the vanguard had already delivered several blows to the enemy but without the presence of the other two factors.'

13 Mario Payeras, *Los días de la selva* ('Days of the Jungle', Monthly Review Press, 1983) and *El trueno en la cuidad* ('The Thunder in the city', 1987).

14 See *Dissidence, Révolution, Lutte armée et Terrorisme*, vol 1 (L'Harmattan, 2006).

15 This is notably the theme of recent texts by Balibar.

16 The debate about non-violence in Rifondazione Comunista's theoretical review (Alternative) is certainly not without a bearing on its present course.

17 Notably Mandel's, in his polemics against the eurocommunists' theses. See his book in the Maspero little collection and above all his interview in *Critique Communiste*.

18 The experience of the participatory budget at the Rio Grande do Sol state level offers many concrete examples in this respect: credit allocation, ranking of priorities, territorial sharing of collective supplies, etc.

19 It may be worth coming back to a discussion of this notion of a united front, or *a fortiori* the anti-imperialist united front which some revolutionaries in Latin America have made flavour of the month, in the light of the evolution of social formations, of the role and composition of political parties, etc.

20 At stake here, as far as the orientation in Brazil is concerned, was a conception of the Fourth International and its relationship to the national sections. But this question goes beyond the context of this text.

21 See Carl Schmitt, *La Dictature* (Paris, 1990).

22 By 'traditional' does Sitel mean communist parties or, more broadly, social democratic parties whose aim is the conquest of governmental power through parliamentary means?

23 See the book by Fausto Bertinotti, *Ces idées qui ne meurent jamais* (Paris, Le temps des Cerises, 2001), and critical approach to it (which appeared at the time of the ESF in Florence) in Daniel Bensaïd, *Un monde à changer* (Paris, Textuel, 2003).

Daniel Bensaïd
The party and the period

The following interview with Daniel Bensaïd was conducted during the Ernest Mandel Symposium held in Brussels on November 19th, 2005. Bensaïd outlines his views on the role of a revolutionary organisation in the present period and recalls his first encounters with Ernest Mandel. The interview appeared in the January 2006 issue of La Gauche, which is published by the LCR-SAP (Belgian section of the Fourth International).

La Gauche: Some people are talking about a new kind of organization, a new kind of party. What do you think about it?

Daniel Bensaïd: Today, a party, in its organisation and in its internal life, has to take into account the diversity of social movements. It can benefit from technological advances: a telephone conference, exchanges on the Internet, which can facilitate horizontal exchanges... That is already very important because one of the powers of bureaucracies was the monopoly of information and of the transmission of information. We are far from the vertical and military conception of the party.

Delimitation in relation to social movements is a condition for respecting these movements and their autonomy. It is less manipulative than hiding inside them and it also respects democratic life within the political organisations and parties themselves. If we have debates, congresses, if we make the effort to produce bulletins, to exchange contradictory positions, there has to be something at stake, otherwise it is democracy without an objective.

The objective concerns major questions. We are not going fight to the death over questions of local tactics. We can have various kinds of agreements on electoral tactics, when a local branch wants to try out something that is not within the framework of the general orientation at national level.

The famous democratic centralism is often criticised, because we have an image of the way it was practised by bureaucratic organisations. But by approaching the question in this way we forget that centralism and democracy are not antinomies, but that each is the condition of the other. We conduct a democratic debate with the aim of taking decisions to which we are all committed.

I think – I don't know if we'll always avoid this – that what has particularly enabled the LCR to avoid up to now the crises that have destroyed other organisations, is that we didn't have the pretension of founding a theoretical orthodoxy. From the beginning, at the end of the 1960s, there were among us followers of Althusser and Sartre, there were Mandelites, and obviously there is no question of a congress voting on the law of value or on the Freudian unconscious. We agree on tasks, on the interpretation of events and common political tasks. There is a whole space for debate.

A revolutionary party can be the bearer of historic memory, but that does not prevent it from missing out on things, for example on ecology. How can we act today so as to not miss out on the movement of ethnic minorities or the revolt in the suburbs?

Every continuity can lead to a certain type of conservatism. There can also be a religion of memory. For me, political memory is necessary, and it is all the more important for the oppressed, who do not have the same institutions to perpetuate memory as the ruling classes do. For the ruling classes, memory is passed on by a whole series of state institutions, and there is a memory of struggles, of the oppressed, of the defeated, which is carried forward by revolutionary organisations.

We have to deal with what is new, but we do not deal with it starting from nothing. The real problem is to know whether we are capable of welcoming what is new without making it fit into the repetition of what we already know. That is the challenge. When we say "we were late, we missed the rendezvous", yes again. But precise rendezvous, even in love, are somewhat rare.

I make less use of the term vanguard, because the notion has a military connotation that can create confusion. It is rather a question of a metabolism, of an exchange between the social movements and the political struggle. It would be paradoxical to have a certain idea of the vanguard as being more 'advanced' than the masses, and then reproaching it with not having invented feminism or ecology. It is after all quite normal that it should come in the first place from social processes on a mass scale, which are then expressed on the political level.

On the other hand today in France we can see very well the specific function of he party. That is why there is for me a 'comeback' (of politics). We have had years of social resistance since the end of the 1980s. We almost had, given the bankruptcy of the policies of reform and of the revolutions of the 20th century, illusions in the self-sufficiency of social movements.

They are necessary, everything starts from there, but everything doesn't finish there. We can see the repeated waves of struggle in Argentina, in Bolivia. If that does not lead to a transformation at every level, including on the level of the structures of power, it becomes an endless, infernal repetition. You overthrow three governments in Bolivia, two in Argentina and afterwards you are still where you were before.

So we have to pose the problem in these terms. During the presidential campaign in France, we are going to ask the social movements for a position on feminism, we are going to ask the ecology movement for a position on energies of substitution. At a meeting in Brest, our candidate, Olivier Besancenot, is asked about his position on the size of fishing nets. He can say: "I don't know everything, I have no opinion about that".

We are a political organisation which seeks to offer an orientation to the country as a whole, but the political organisations and the different social movements are obliged to synthesise at least the answers to the big questions. Today, that is the difficulty that an organisation like ATTAC is experiencing. It is very good that ATTAC is a unitary organisation, an organisation for popular education, but we clearly saw, when we got to the European referendum, that it was the political organisations that were the moving force of the mobilisation.

I think that we are at a turning point, the moment of transition from one cycle to another. We saw it with the German elections. We will see it again with the Italian elections, we will see what happens politically afterwards. Because resistance is a pre-condition that is necessary but not sufficient. If we want to respect the autonomy of the mass movements, then paradoxically, political organisations are necessary. Obviously, we need to have created a culture of pluralism, of respect, but at the same time, we have to firmly defend political positions.

We are also emerging from a period where the key word is consensus. To defend your convictions is not necessarily authoritarian. If you do it correctly, it is rather an expression of respect for others. If you are convinced of what you think, you try to convince others of it, because they are not any more stupid than you, they can reach the same conclusions.

By discussing seriously with others, we also run the risk of being convinced by them. That is in fact the logic of a real debate. On that point, Ernest Mandel was not at all sectarian, but he was very convinced of and very firm about his own positions. That is better than defending sloppy ideas.

My first encounter with Ernest Mandel was here in Brussels: at a meeting during May '68. The meeting had been banned, but I had not been stopped at the border, because I arrived from the Ardennes. Cohn-Bendit had been turned back. It was already a pluralist meeting, because Cohn-Bendit was an anarchist; as for me, I can't say I was a Trotskyist, I was more a Guevarist.

The meeting was finally besieged by the police, who succeeded in getting hold of me and taking me back to the border. It was my first contact with Ernest, but it was ephemeral, because I was immediately kicked out of Belgium. Afterwards we did in fact meet on many occasions. I would like to say that the contact was quite affectionate and respectful. We never had the cult of the personality.

Perhaps we were arrogant and insufferable, because we were young cocks. At the age of 20 we thought we had started a revolution. We discussed on what was really quite an equal footing. Ernest did not entirely persuade us when he tried to convince us to join the Fourth International on the basis of a rather favourable presentation of what forces it had. Well, it wasn't very convincing, because there weren't many forces.

We were more convinced by logical reasoning: the world was – less than today – globalised, an International was necessary, there is one, it isn't what we wanted, but it is very honourable, it hasn't betrayed, it fought Stalinism, so let's go, and it will change with us. We will contribute to its transformation.

At the end of the day, Ernest underestimated the strength of logical arguments. That was unusual for him. He had great confidence in the power of ideas, but he tried to convince me on the basis of the material force of the Fourth International, which was relatively modest. But it worked all the same.

Daniel Bensaid
'Leninism' and party organisation in the 21st Century

Interview by Phil Hearse, 2001

PH: Lenin made important contributions to Marxist thinking about imperialism, the national question, revolutionary strategy and socialist democracy. But when parties and groups call themselves 'Leninist' they are generally referring to organisational forms. Yet the modern experience of such organisations has shown they have quite diverse organisational practices. What is special about 'Leninism' as an organisational form?

DB: We have to start by remembering that the very term 'Leninism' only appeared after the death of Lenin, notably in the speech by Zinoviev to the Fifth Congress of the Communist International (1924). It corresponds to the codification of an organisational model then associated with the 'Bolshevisation' of the Comintern, which allowed the Kremlin to brutally subjugate the young Communist parties to its own tutelage, in the name of combating social democracy – which had been corrupted by parliamentarism.

The invention of 'Leninism' as a religiously mummified orthodoxy, was part of the process of bureaucratisation of the Comintern and the Soviet Union. That's why, as far as possible, I personally avoid utilising this 'ism'. However, if you attempt to summarise what appears essential in Lenin's own organisational ideas, I would highlight two ideas which seem to me essential revolutionary conceptions for this epoch, and which retain their validity today.

The first, which was at the centre of the polemic in What is to Be Done, and in One Step Forward, Two Steps Back, is the distinction between the (revolutionary) party and the (working) class, which rejects all confusionist attempts to conflate or identify the two. This distinction, elementary from the point of view of the Marxism of the Second International, implies thinking through the specificity of the political field, its relationship of forces, and its own concepts.

This terrain is not simply a reflection or an extension of the social relationship of forces. It expresses the transformation of the social relations (and class struggle) into political terms, with its own – as the psychoanalysts say – displacements and condensations. I would above all highlight that this distinction between the social and the political, between parties and classes, paradoxically opens up the possibility of thinking through the idea of pluralism; if the party is not simply the incarnation of the class, not simply a one-to-one expression of its social substance, then it becomes thinkable that the party can be represented by a plurality of parties.

As a corollary the class can build instruments of resistance independent of parties. Thus it doesn't seem to me accidental that Lenin had the most correct position during the early 1920s debate in Russia on the role of the trade unions.

The second essential idea is in relation to what appears to be one of the most debatable characteristics of Leninism, democratic centralism. To the extent that this idea became associated with the bureaucratic centralism of the Stalinist period, what one remembers above all is centralism and the image of a semi-military discipline.

Thus, for us the democratic aspect is fundamental. If, after free discussion, there doesn't exist a collective effort and a mutual involvement in putting all the decisions to the test of practice, the democracy of an organisation remains purely formal and 'parliamentary'. It becomes reduced to an exchange of opinions without real consequences, everyone can participate in the debate with their own convictions, without a common practice to test the validity of a political orientation.

PH: How has the LCR's conception of Leninism evolved since its founding conference in 1969?

DB: Because of the strong spontaneist illusions which the May 1968 movement in France engendered among the youth, the foundation of the Ligue Communiste as a section of the Fourth International in 1969 was the result of a lively debate, notably on the question of organisation. With more than 30 years of hindsight, this founding debate seems to me decisive. It permitted us to create an organisation which resisted the retreat after 1968, and survived the test of subsequent defeats.

However, a critical review of that period is necessary. In the context of the period, we had a tendency to fetishise the party as the direct and immediate adversary of the state (inspired by a questionable reading of

Poulantzas), and gave our 'Leninism' a slightly 'militarist' twist ('ultra-left' if you prefer). In this you can see the influence of Guevara, his voluntarism and the role attributed to 'exemplary' actions.

In that sense, our interpretation partially created a sort of 'forced Leninism', criticised by Regis Debray in his book A Critique of Arms.

PH: For more than a decade we have seen groups which refer to Leninism operating inside quite broad formations like the PT in Brazil, the PRC in Italy and now we have the experience of the Scottish Socialist Party. Isn't there a danger that prolonged immersion in these parties will atrophy the political independence of such Leninist groups, and adversely affect there ability to operate as a coherent striking force in times of political crisis?

DB: The examples mentioned in the question represent different experiences of party construction, each one different in its context, each one specific – from the birth of a mass workers party (Brazil), to the conflicts within the old Communist parties (Italy), to regroupments of radical currents.

Beyond that, despite this diversity, these experiences are embedded in a situation of redefinition and political recomposition, opened by the end of the 'short 20th century' since the fall of the Berlin Wall and the disintegration of the Soviet Union. This is only the beginning of a long period of mutation and redefinition of the forces within the progressive social movements.

The idea of a 'prolonged immersion' doesn't seem to me appropriate to talk about these experiences, to the extent that it seems to evoke the experiences of 'entrism' in the mass workers parties, in the 1930s or after the second world war. There's nothing 'entrist' about the presence of revolutionary currents in the Brazilian Workers Party (PT). They participate in a process of pluralist party construction, rather similar to the mass workers parties before the first world war (where the notion of entrism also had no sense).

Within these experiences there are contradictions which we must recognise and engage. A party like the Brazilian PT is subject to strong pressures, because its presence in parliament and role in local and regional governments. At the same time, this enables the accumulation of social experiences on a grand scale. Does this mean that a revolutionary current risks blunting its cutting edge and losing its revolutionary spirit? Without doubt. But on the other hand, if a revolutionary current remains separate it also risks losing its revolutionary soul, and becoming simply a sect which denounces, without getting its hands dirty.

Between the two risks it is necessary to choose, looking for the best solutions to the dangers (like the education of militants) knowing there are no absolute guarantees.

In any case, every organisation creates conservative tendencies (including the Bolshevik party in 1917) and nobody can be sure of being up to the job if there is a revolutionary crisis; the crisis itself is a test of the validity of a construction project, and the verdict is not known in advance.

PH: Why, in principle, should capitalism not be overthrown by an alliance of mass social movements, each of which is organised around partial emancipatory projects – especially if they all see capitalism as the enemy?

DB: The question doesn't seem to me to be the best way to approach it. From a certain point of view, capitalism will indeed be overthrown by an alliance, or a convergence, of mass social movements. But even if these movements, because of their liberatory projects, perceive capitalism to be their enemy (which perhaps is the case for the women's movement or the environmental movement, not just the workers movement), I don't think these movements all play an equivalent role. And all are traversed by differences and contradictions which reflect their position, in the face of capital as a global mode of domination.

There is a 'naturalist' feminism and a revolutionary feminism, a profoundly anti-humanist environmentalism and a humanist and social environmentalism. In discussing this, one could perhaps integrate the sociological contributions of Max Weber and Pierre Bourdieu on the growing social differentiation of modern society and the diversity of its social arenas. If you consider theses arenas are not structured in a hierarchy, but simply juxtaposed, then perhaps you could devise a tactic of putting together changing coalitions ('rainbow coalitions' on immediate questions). But there would be no solid strategic convergence in such an approach.

I think, on the contrary, that within a particular mode of production (capitalism), relations of exploitation and class conflict constitute an overarching framework which cuts across and unifies the other contradictions. Capital itself is the great unifier which subordinates every aspect of social production and reproduction, remodelling the function of the family, determining the social division of labour and submitting humanity's conditions of social reproduction to the law of value. If that is indeed the case, a party, and not simply the sum of social movements, is the best agent of conscious unification,.

PH: The foundation of Lenin's post-1914 strategy was that imperialism was in its 'death agony', and was by definition a period of capitalist decline. How does this stand up after nine decades?

DB: I don't interpret that characterisation of the epoch, an epoch of wars and revolutions, as a conjunctural judgement, or a mechanical judgement about the inevitable collapse of the system. Retrospectively, the 20th century does indeed appear to have been the century of wars and revolutions. And the 21st century, alas, won't be any different from that point of view. The forms of imperialist domination change but they don't disappear. The relevance of the heritage of Lenin and Trotsky, understood in a critical and non-dogmatic way, resides in the contemporary reality of capital and imperialism itself.

PH: Several revolutionary organisations outside the Fourth International (for example LO, the SWP and the DSP) tend to argue that the French LCR is badly organised and lacks political centralisation. Do you agree that the LCR's deep and permanent involvement in diverse mass movements and united fronts has reduced its capacity for rapid mobilisation around central campaigns. And if so, is this an inevitable choice in modern conditions?

DB: There's an element of truth in that. The LCR was able to resist the defeats of the 1980s and 90s essentially thanks to its activity in the mass movement – in the trade unions and in the mass social movements (unemployed, women and anti-racist). Everyone recognises in France that the renewal of fighting trade unionism, or that of AC and Ras L'Front (1), couldn't have seen the same level of development without the militants of the LCR.

But the framework of a weakening in workers' resistance, the usefulness of the mass social movements seemed more obvious than that of a political organisation like ours, which could appear at a certain point just as a network and a forum for discussing ideas.

This certainly led to an organisational loosening, which we regret and have been trying to correct for several years, say since 1995-7. But we prefer that problem to being a 'besieged citadel'. Lutte Ouvriere (Workers Struggle) has certainly maintained a higher level of party patriotism, but the price has been exorbitant; a sectarian petrification and an incomprehension of the social movements.

Then again, there is always a tension between the building of a political party and intervention in united fronts, between the risk of a sectarian response and that of dilution of your political profile. One can't resist that double temptation by a magic formula, you have to work your way though it concretely in each case.

In a demonstration LO (if it participates) can have a contingent numerically bigger than the Ligue's, but the militants of the Ligue are also present in the contingents of their trade unions, Attac, Ras L'Front etc. I think we do more to develop the 'real movement for the abolition of the existing order', which is the very definition of communism.

PH: The recent well-attended SWP school 'Marxism 2001' showed again that the age profile of far left organisations in Europe is not so good (the majority more than 30, with a high proportion more than 40). Why? What can be done about it?

DB: What strikes me and seems most important, more than the age profile than summer schools and meetings like the Marx conferences in France, is the renewal of interest in the Marxist critique of modern society and capitalist globalisation. Certainly, we would prefer a younger attendance, but the fact that a part of the 1960s generation has politically survived the 'Thatcher years' or the 'Mitterrand years' is something of a bonus for the future; there's the possibility of a continuity and a transmission of experiences. Basing ourselves on that we have to make an effort to find the way to access the present forms of politicisation of young people. For these certainly exist.

In the present mobilisations against globalisations we can see parallels with the struggles which generated the radicalisation before 1968 – like over Vietnam or the Algerian war. We shouldn't mythologise or exaggerate that pre-1968 radicalisation, by the way.

We can also see the present radicalisation in musical or cultural phenomena. On the other hand, if organisations like the SWP and LCR are a bit 'hollowed out' as regards the 1980s generation, they seem to understand the beginning of a new perspective among the youth.

PH: It was an axiom for Trotskyist organisations in the 60s, 70s and 80s that Leninism means a permanently high level of activity from all members. Often this involved moralistic and even quasi-religious overtones. Is it realistic to expect large number of activists to sustain high levels of activity for decades? Irrespective of the political situation?

DB: A (voluntary) involvement in revolutionary struggle certainly isn't a hobby for the weekend. It seems normal that it implies a commitment to activity, career sacrifices and financial effort. It's not necessary to achieve that by cultivating a self-sacrificing mystique or the religious spirit of missionaries. Moreover the organisations which practice such ideological doping are often revealed as the most vulnerable to demoralisation; the disillusionment and discouragement are then proportional to the euphoric exaggeration of its motivation. Without doubt the kind of activism often used in the 1970s was often linked to an exaggerated appreciation of the chances for socialists, but also linked to the availability of members who in their overwhelming majority came from the youth, and were not yet inserted in a work or family situation. We say that we have matured and that our militancy has been 'normalised' in the rhythms and needs. The risk could be from now on the reverse: to fall into routinism.

PH: Is democratic centralism a realisable objective on an international level? Are we ever going to see a new mass International organised like the Comintern? In the light of modern experience, is it really true that revolutionary organisations inevitably suffer 'national communist' deviations from being outside an International?

DB: We saw earlier that the notion of democratic centralism is difficult to define. This is all the more so at an international level. The Fourth International was defined at its inception as a world party. This engendered confusion in allowing the view that it was possible to operate with the degree of centralisation of a national party. That permitted misadventures like that of 1952, when the elected leadership of the French section was suspended by the International Secretariat. Such a thing is unimaginable today. The Statutes adopted in 1974 recognised the sovereignty of national leaderships. The 1985 Congress made explicit that the International is composed of sections and not individual adherents, and that implies a very federal structure.

It is necessary to continue the reflection about the type of democracy possible at an international level. If it is possible to adopt common positions about great international events, it is however absurd for European delegates to vote on electoral tactics in Peru or trade union tactics in Brazil. Rather than discuss a formula (world party, democratic centralism), it would perhaps be better now to discuss a calm and objective balance sheet of experiences and practices, to look for the right balance between a destructive over-centralisation and a simple network for discussion, without any common commitment or involvement. It is necessary also to follow attentively the experiences of internationalist renewal, notably in the movement against capitalist globalisation, taking up the discussion of past experiences. I remain personally very attached to the necessity of an International, and I don't think that it is necessary solely during periods of impetuous revolutionary advance. However I don't think the Comintern any longer is a model for this.

PH: The tiny groups fighting to build Leninist parties made their first breakthroughs in the mid-late 1960s. After more than 30 years effort it could be argued that the results are quite modest. Doubtless much of the reason for this is rooted in deep objective factors – defeats of the working class, neoliberalism, the collapse of 'communism' etc. In retrospect, were major mistakes made? Could the results have been better?

DB: The results could no doubt have been better. One could review the history of the 1930s and make an inventory of the mistakes. In fact it's not a useless thing to do at all, because these experiences, these treasures of intelligence, of devotion and of sacrifice were not at all pointless.

But if you consider that the results were limited, with so many avenues explored, so many theoretical interpretations attempted, then without doubt the circumstances were very hard. I say the circumstances and not the objective conditions. For there is a [vice] in the counterposition between objective and subjective conditions. The two are obviously linked. If you completely dissociate them, you fall into paradoxes which have often has disastrous consequences in the Trotskyist movement. If the objective circumstances were as excellent as one thinks, and if the revolutionary movement couldn't capitalise on them, then it was the organisations, their leaderships, their militants who failed; or else there were internal traitors. That type of paranoia does nobody any good.

John Holloway
The concept of power and the Zapatistas

March 1996

1. "A new lie is sold to us as history. The lie about the defeat of hope, the lie about the defeat of dignity, the lie about the defeat of humanity." (Subcomandante Marcos in the invitation to an Intercontinental Gathering against Neo-Liberalism, La Jornada, 30/1/96).

The lie is a lie about power, and about necessity. After twenty years of neo-liberalism, it is no longer really a lie about desirability. The market optimism of the 80s has been largely replaced by a market realism: not "everything is perfect under a market system", but "this is the way things are and this is the way things must be, in reality there is no alternative". "A different society might be nice, but it is not possible." The lie about the defeat of hope is a lie about the defeat of possibility, a lie about the power to change.

The Zapatistas have a different idea of possibility, a different idea of power. This was expressed by Marcos in a comment on the dialogue between the Zapatistas and the government. "This is not a fair dialogue, it is not a dialogue between equals. But in this dialogue the EZLN is not the weak party, it is the strong party. On the side of the government there are only military force and the lies spread by some of the media. And force and lies will never, never be stronger than reason. They can impose themselves for days, months or years, but history will finally put each one in its place" (Subcomandante Marcos, 5/5/95, La Jornada, 11/5/95).

Very pretty, but it's absurd! How can Marcos's declaration possibly be correct? His reference to history does not answer anything, since history is no more than the result of struggles about power. So how can we possibly maintain that the Zapatistas are stronger than the Mexican government, or that reason is stronger than force and lies? To defend such an absurd statement, it would be necessary to defend an absurd theory of power.

That is surely the challenge of the Zapatistas and their absurd rebellion. The Zapatista rebellion is absurd. After the fall of the Berlin Wall, after the defeat of the Sandinistas, after the defeat of the revolutions in El Salvador and Guatemala, when China is becoming more and more integrated into the capitalist world market, when the Cuban revolution is finding it increasingly difficult to survive in any form at all, when all the major revolutionary movements have disappeared from Latin America and most other parts of the world, on the very day that Mexico proclaims its modernity through the creation of the NAFTA, on that very day a group of indigenous peasants seize control of San Cristobal and other towns in Chiapas, many of them armed with wooden guns. Not only that, but they soon proclaim their absurd notions openly: they, a group of a few thousand indigenous rebels in the jungle of the south-east of Mexico want to change the world. What is more, most absurd of all, most important, most central to their whole absurd project, they want to change the world without taking power. And on top of that their discourse is full of jokes, of stories, of children, of dancing. How can we take such a rebellion seriously? It all seems too much of a colourful tale from a novel by Gabriel Garcia Marquez for it to be of serious relevance to us here in Europe.

I want to take the Zapatistas seriously. I want Marcos to be right when he says that they are stronger than the Mexican government. I want them to be right when they say that they want to change the world without taking power. I want them to be right because I do not see any other way out of the tragedy we are living, in which about 50,000 people die each day of starvation, in which over a thousand million people live in extreme poverty. Revolution is desperately urgent, but often it appears that we are trapped in a desperately urgent impossibility. I want Marcos's declarations to be not only beautiful and poetic but to have a real theoretical and practical foundation. But wanting them to be right is not enough. If we want them to be right, we must try to understand, criticise and strengthen the theoretical and practical foundation of what they are doing.

The Zapatistas pose a theoretical and practical challenge: a challenge to all the established practices and ideas of the revolutionary left or indeed of the Left in the broadest sense. As Marcos puts it in a comment on the first year of the uprising, "Something broke in this year, not just the false image of modernity sold to us by neoliberalism, not just the falsity of government projects, of institutional alms, not just the unjust neglect by the country of its original inhabitants, but also the rigid schemes of a Left living in and from the past. In the midst of this navigating from pain to hope, political struggle finds itself naked, bereft of the rusty garb inherited from pain: it is hope which obliges it to look for new forms of struggle, that is, new ways of being political, of doing politics: a new politics, a new political morality, a new political ethic is not just a wish, it is the only way to go forward, to jump to the other side". (Subcommandante Marcos – cited by Rosario Ibarra, La Jornada, 2/5/95). He might also have added, "a new political theory, a new understanding of politics and of power".

2. Power is usually associated with control of money or the state. The left, in particular, has usually seen social transformation in terms of control of the state. The strategies of the mainstream left have generally aimed at winning control of the state and using the state to transform society. The reformist left sees gaining control of the state in terms of winning elections, the revolutionary left (certainly in the Leninist and 'guerrillero' traditions) thinks of it in terms of the seizure of state power. The classic controversies between reformists and revolutionaries have been about the means of winning control of the state. The actual goal of taking state power is generally taken as an obvious prerequisite for changing society.

The attempts to transform society through the state (whether by reformist or revolutionary means) have never achieved what they set out to do. So many historical failures cannot be accounted for in terms of 'betrayal' of the revolution or of the people. The failure of so many attempts to use state power suggests rather that the state is not the site of power. States are embedded in a world-wide web of capitalist social relations that defines their character. States are incapable of bringing about radical social change simply because the flight of capital which any such attempt would cause would threaten the very existence of the state. The notion of state power is a mirage: the seizure of the state is not the seizure of power.

The attempts to transform society through the state have not just failed to achieve that end. The fixation on the state has tended to destroy the movements pushing for radical change. If states are embedded in a global web of capitalism, that means that they tend to reproduce capitalist social relations through the way that they operate. States function in such a way as to reproduce the capitalist status quo. In their relation to us, and in our relation to them, there is a filtering out of anything that is not compatible with the reproduction of capitalist social relations. This may be a violent filtering, as in the repression of revolutionary or subversive activity, but it is also a less perceptible filtering, a sidelining or suppression of passions, loves, hates, anger, laughter, dancing. The state divides the public from the private and, in so doing, imposes a division upon us, separates our public, serious side from our private, frivolous, irrelevant side. The state fragments us, alienates us from ourselves.

The problem with any left activity oriented towards the state is that it tends to reproduce the same fragmentation of the person. If power is identified with the state, then winning power is identified with the suppression of part of ourselves: with seriousness, dedication, sacrifice, the elimination of all 'irresponsibility'. In the case of reformist political parties which are oriented to winning control of the state by electoral means, the nature of the state's insertion in capitalist social relations means that there are considerable pressures on the party to project itself as serious, responsible and respectful of property, and to suppress any rank-and-file activity which does not correspond to this image. Revolutionaries do not produce the image of the state in quite the same way, but, especially where conditions are such as to make any revolutionary organisation clandestine, a revolutionary must be prepared to dedicate himself, to sacrifice, to subordinate his life to the higher goal of winning power. Although the aim may be to create a society in which the person would be whole, in which alienation would be overcome, it is assumed that in the meantime the winning of power requires the fragmentation of oneself. It is assumed that in a nasty, alienated society, the only way of taking on the enemy is to adopt the enemy's language and forms of organisation.

This way of looking at power has its most extreme expression in the identification of power with military force. The army (whether state or revolutionary) is not only a model for factory organisation but its exaggeration, the intensification of self-alienation to its extreme, the maximum subordination of normal affective life. In the idea that power is military force (and that power must be won by military force), power and dehumanisation (of self and others) are treated as practically identical.

The state-oriented tradition of organisation privileges men (and especially young men), not necessarily in the sense of any direct discrimination against women, but above all in the way that different forms of social experience are valued. Professional dedication to the revolution promotes a culture in which there is a hierarchisation of social experience and activity. Action or experience directed at the state is given priority, and other types of experience (affective relations, playing with children, sensuality etc) are accorded a secondary importance. The same separation between the public and the private, between the serious and the frivolous, which is the basis of the existence of the state, is reproduced within the revolutionary (or reformist) organisation. In the capitalist world, politics is a serious (not to say boring) business, a matter above all for the serious (not to say boring) gender, a matter that has no room for children, jokes or games. In the world of the traditional left, it is not very different.

3. If it is correct to see the idea of the revolutionary seizure of state power as an idea particularly suited to the experience of young single people, then it is easy to understand why the Zapatistas abandoned their traditional notions of revolution as they became transformed from a revolutionary group into a community in arms. They have repeatedly said that they do not want to conquer state power. Time and time again, in their practice and in their declarations, they have rejected the state as a form of action.

The most fundamental example of their rejection of the state as a form of organisation is their insistence on the principle of 'mandar obedeciendo', 'lead by obeying', the idea that the leaders of the movement must obey the members, and that all major decisions should be taken through a process of collective decision making. This principle has meant constant friction in the dialogue with the government, as can be seen for example in the conflict over the issue of time. Given the bad conditions of communication in the Lacandona Jungle, and the need to discuss everything thoroughly, the principle of 'mandar obedeciendo' means that decisions take time. When the government representatives insisted on rapid replies, the Zapatistas replied that they did not understand the indigenous clock. As recounted by Comandante David afterwards, the Zapatistas explained that "we, as Indians, have rhythms, forms of understanding, of deciding, of reaching agreements. And when we told them that, they replied by making fun of us; well then, they said, we don't understand why you say that because we see that you have Japanese watches, so how do you say that you are wearing indigenous watches, that's from Japan." (La Jornada, 17/5/95). And Comandante Tacho commented: "They haven't learned. They understand us backwards. We use time, not the clock." (La Jornada, 18/5/95).

The rejection of the state is central also to the Zapatistas' relations with 'civil society'. All their strategies to build a unity of action with those engaged in other forms of struggle quite explicitly bypass the state. Most recently, in the Fourth Declaration of the Lacandona Jungle, issued at the beginning of this year, in which they propose the formation of a Front of National Liberation, they make it an explicit condition for joining this front that members should renounce all aspiration to hold state office – an idea which has scandalised sympathisers both on the reformist and the trotskyist left.

4. But then what? The Zapatistas say that they do not want to conquer the world, just to make it new. But that implies some concept of strength or

power. If power is not defined as the state, or as military force, then what is the alternative? How can we think of the power of those without power, the face of those without face, the voice of those without voice?

The Zapatistas speak of what they say as the "word of those who are armed with truth and fire" ("la palabra de los armados de verdad y fuego"). The fire is there, but the truth comes first, not just as a moral attribute, but as a weapon: they are armed with truth, and this is a more important weapon than the firepower of their guns. Although they are organised as an army, they aim to win by truth, not by fire.

Those "without voice, without face" are armed with truth. Their truth is not just that they speak the truth about their situation or about the country, but that they are true to themselves. Truth is dignity, having the dignity to say at last the 'Enough!' that would restore meaning to the deaths of their dead. Dignity is to assert one's humanity in a society which treats us inhumanly. Dignity is to assert our wholeness in a society which fragments us. Dignity is to assert control over one's life in a society which denies such control. Dignity is to live in the present the Not Yet for which we struggle. To be armed with truth or dignity is to assert the power of living now that which is not yet.

In the assertion that they/we are armed with truth or dignity, the conventional concept of power is reversed. Power is not that which is , but that which is not, that which is Not Yet (as Bloch would put it). In a society in which that which is ("that's the way things are") rules, in which identity is lord, to be armed with dignity is to assert the power of non-identity. In a society based on human alienation, the Zapatistas raise the banner of non-alienation, of that which is suppressed, of laughing, singing and dancing, of that which simply does not appear in the normal categories of social science, constructed as they are on the basis of the Is-ness or identity of the world.

But is this not empty, metaphysical nonsense? How can one speak of the power of that which is not yet, of non-alienation, of non-identity, of dignity and truth? History is littered with the corpses of the true and dignified, and ultimately powerless.

The appeal to that which is Not Yet would be purely metaphysical if the Not Yet did not exist in some form already. The appeal to a pre-given History, or to some Dignity, understood as a pre-given Platonic essence, does not help at all. It is only if we understand dignity, truth, non-identity, the Not Yet as already existing that we can begin to think of power in those terms. They exist, of course, not as transcendent essences, but as present

134

refusal, as struggle, as negation of the untruth of capitalist society. Truth exists as stuggle against untruth, dignity as struggle against degradation, non-alienation as struggle against alienation, non-identity as struggle against identity, the not-yet as struggle against the present. In short, they exist as the !Ya Basta! [That's Enough! – ed] inside all of us. This is expressed very nicely by Antonio Garcia de Leon in his prologue to one of the editions of the Zapatista communiques, where he says "as more and more rebel communiques were issued, we realised that in reality the revolt came from the depths of ourselves". The power of the Zapatistas is the power of the !Ya Basta!, the negation of oppression, which exists in the depths of all of us.

How do we know that the !Ya Basta! exists? We know it must exist in all of us, possibly very suppressed, always in contradictory form, but always there, not just from experience, but simply because it is an inseparable part of life in an oppressive society. We can see manifestations of it in the million different struggles that make up life in a capitalist society, from the strikes that shook France at the end of last year to the cursing of the alarm clock that tells us it is time to go to an alienating job in the mornings. But there is no way it can be measured, no way in which we can empirically define it. The fact that it exists in often unarticulated form means that there is an irreducible unpredictability in social development.

The question of the power of the Zapatistas can now be reformulated as the question of how we articulate the !Ya Basta! – not their !Ya Basta! but our !Ya basta! If we think of their power in this sense, it helps us to understand why the Zapatistas have not (or not yet) been suppressed militarily: it is not due primarily to their military strength, but to the extraordinary resonance of their !Ya Basta! in Mexico and throughout the world.

Thinking of the issue of power in this way also helps us to understand aspects of the Zapatistas' politics. The understanding of people as already having dignity in a society which degrades them, as already having truth in an untrue society (truth and dignity not as essential qualities but as negation of degradation and untruth) is the crucial turning point in their concept of revolution. Understanding people as having dignity implies a politics of listening and not just talking (a politics of mutual recognition). Through the process of being integrated into the communities of the Lacandona Jungle, the original group of revolutionaries were forced to listen in order to communicate, they were forced to abandon the great revolutionary tradition of talking, of telling people what to think. Revolutionary politics then becomes the articulation of Dignity's struggle, rather than the bringing of class consciousness to the people from outside. From this follow two of the key phrases of the Zapatista discourse – 'mandar obedeciendo' (to lead by obeying) and 'preguntando caminamos' (asking we walk). Revolution is redefined as a question rather than an answer: revolution is "revolution with a small 'r'", rather than Revolution with a capital R. It refers to the creative and imaginative articulation of dignity now, and not to a future event, the arrival at a pre-defined promised land.

The notion of dignity and of listening to people's struggles also helps to explain why the Zapatistas do not call for supporters to come and join them in the jungle, but insist rather that people should struggle wherever they are in whatever way they can. In effect they say not "we are right, join us", but "we must all struggle to express our !Ya Basta!". The various political initiatives they have taken – the National Democratic Convention in Aguascalientes, the national and international consultations on the aims and future of the Zapatistas, the movement of national liberation, the indigenous forum, and now the intercontinental gathering against neo-liberalism – all aim, not at building up their own membership, nor at constructing a solidarity movement, but at stimulating others to strengthen their own struggles for democracy, freedom and justice.

Their appeal is a general one, to what they call 'civil society'. They do not talk either of class struggle or of the proletariat. This has been criticised by some Marxists as reformist, but, although the concept of 'civil society' is unsatisfactory in some respects, it is understandable why the Zapatistas should prefer to avoid the vocabulary of the Marxist tradition, laden as it is with a hundred years of positivist interpretation. The concept of the proletariat is particularly problematic. As usually understood, it refers to a particular group of people defined by a particular type of subjection to capital. As such, it privileges the struggles of certain people over others and certain types of struggle over others. The Zapatistas' concept of !Ya basta!, on the other hand, more in keeping with Marx's own work, it seems to me, can be seen as based on the idea that the class antagonism runs through all of us, although in different ways, and as allowing a much richer concept of struggle as embracing all aspects of human activity.

In the past two years, this group of rebels in the jungle of the south-east of Mexico, born of the interaction of a group of revolutionaries with the traditions of struggle of the indigenous people of Chiapas, born in the 1990s of the horrors of world neo-liberalism which force so many people either to die in misery or to say "!Ya Basta!", has crystallised (and advanced) to a remarkable extent the themes of oppositional thought and action that have been discussed throughout the world in recent years: the issues of gender, age, childhood, death and the dead. All flow from the understanding of politics as a politics of dignity, a politics which recognises the particular oppression of, and respects the struggles of, women, children, the old. Respect for the struggles of the old is a constant theme of Marcos's stories, particularly through the figure of Old Antonio, but was also forcefully underlined by the emergence of Comandante Trinidad as one of the leading figures in the dialogue of San Andres. The way in which women have imposed recognition of their struggles on the Zapatista men is well known, and can be seen, for example, in the Revolutionary Law for Women, issued on the first day of the uprising, or in the fact that it was a woman, Ana Maria, who led the most important military action undertaken by the Zapatistas, the occupation of San Cristobal on the 1st January 1994. The question of childhood and the freedom to play is a constant theme in Marcos's letters and is highlighted in a recent interview as the issue that he regards as most important: "In our dream children are children and their work is to be children... I do not dream of the agrarian redistribution, of big mobilisations, of the fall of the government and elections and the victory of a left-wing party, or whatever. I dream of the children and I see them being children... We, the Zapatista children, think that our work as children is to play and to learn" (interview with Cristian Calonico Lucio, 11/11/95, (not published at the time this article was written -@kör autonomedia)).

It is not that the struggle of the Zapatistas – the military conflict and the prolonged dialogue with the government – has also raised these important issues. Rather these issues are central to the struggle. The struggle is not just about gaining material improvements, better housing, schools, hospitals and so on: it is about creating a world in which people can live with dignity, a mutually recognitive world in which people can relate to each other without hiding behind masks. Seen in this light, the letters of Marcos, the poetry, the theatre of Aguascalientes and the dances that punctuate all that the Zapatistas do are not embellishments of a revolutionary process but central to it.

The question for us, then, is not how we can build solidarity committees, but how we can join in the process that they have started. How can we theorise and articulate our own !Ya Basta!? How can we think about the unity of our particular struggles and the struggles of the other Zapatistas, those in the southeast of Mexico? How can we articulate that unity in a struggle for a society in which dignity would no longer be a struggle against degradation? It is presumably to stir up such questions that the Zapatistas are calling for an Intercontinental Gathering for Humanity and against Neo-Liberalism, to be celebrated between the months of April and August in the five continents .

The Zapatistas, far from being just another rebellion in some far-off land, challenge us theoretically and practically, challenge us to join in the struggle for dignity: dignity, according to Marcos in the declaration calling for the intercontinental gathering, "is that nation without nationality, that rainbow that is also a bridge, that murmur of the heart no matter what blood lives in it, that rebel irreverence that mocks borders, customs and wars".

Preguntando caminamos. Asking we walk.

Phil Hearse
Latin America – resistance and revolution

June 2006

On no continent is neoliberalism so widely rejected as in Latin America, and nowhere has the resurgence of the Left been so powerful. The election of Evo Morales in Bolivia and the evolution of the Hugo Chávez government in Venezuela are hugely ideologically important. Whatever the direction and eventual outcome of these governments, they have already done an enormously important thing – given an arithmetic content to the algebraic formula that 'another world is possible'; the only possible one, socialism.

Even the election of moderate centre-left governments, like those of Lula in Brazil, Bachelet in Chile and Tabaré Vázquez in Uruguay are the product of a long period of struggle against neoliberalism and the right.

The huge Latin American panorama of struggle has given rise to new debates about revolutionary strategy – debates which the left has not been used to having for some time. How can this enormous generation of struggle, the rejection of neoliberalism and the rise of the Left be consolidated into permanent socialist gains, the power of the popular masses and the defeat of capitalism?

Continent wide tactics are useless and Latin American societies are enormously diverse. There is no 'one strategy fits all' solution. However there are common elements in the development of these societies and certain common elements in revolutionary strategy as well.

There are a number of crucial questions, the answers to which will act as crucial guidelines for a revolutionary alternative. They include:

1: What is the nature of these societies and their relationship with imperialism?

2: What is the nature of the ruling class?

3: What is the character of the 'revolutionary subject'? What is the (potential) alliance of popular forces which might be mobilised into an alliance to make a revolutionary breakthrough?

4: What are the key steps needed to make an anti-capitalist transition and a break with the capitalist state and imperialism?

Each of the countries of Latin America is oppressed by imperialism. Semi-industrialisation in Brazil and Argentina means that the countries can no longer be considered as having all the classic characteristics of semi-colonies, ie being providers solely of raw materials and consumers of manufactures from the imperialist centres. Nonetheless, none of them, not even a giant economy like Brazil, is an autonomous centre for the accumulation of finance capital at the same level as the imperialist countries or a centre for multinational corporations which bestride and exploit the world.

The proof of the pudding was the debt crisis; in the worst years of the crisis in the 1980s and 1990s, a huge tribute of capital flowed out of the exploited countries towards the imperialist centres. Brazil and Argentina were of course in the former category, with a decade of economic progress destroyed in the 1980s by the debt crisis. If all the countries of Latin America are dominated by imperialism, then they have a super-rich ruling class which is hand-in-hand with the imperialist bourgeoisie. This has created some of the most unequal societies on earth; in Mexico and Brazil the rich are rich by international standards and the poor are poor by the same standards. The idea that there can be any kind of 'anti-imperialist alliance' with any sector of the bourgeoisie whatever is tremendously far-fetched. At best there can be alliances around democratic objectives and only conjunctural national interests.

In his theory of permanent revolution Trotsky proposed that the working class had to lead the struggle for the national and democratic tasks of the revolution, that is to say unfulfilled tasks of the bourgeois revolution. Trotsky differed with the Stalinists in seeing the national democratic revolution as a phase of an uninterrupted ('permanent') revolutionary process, which would be carried out by an alliance of the working class and the peasantry, under the political leadership of the working class itself. There would be no Chinese wall between the national and democratic tasks and the socialist tasks, and the whole process would require the dictatorship of the working class (and the peasantry).

Insofar as we need to modify Trotsky's theory, which after all was elaborated mainly between 1905 and 1928, it can only be in the direction of stressing the interaction and inter-relatedness of the national democratic tasks and the socialist tasks. To put it another way, to achieve real democracy and real national independence requires a complete break with imperialism and the oligarchy.

For example, for Bolivia to achieve real national independence means taking control of its own resources: ie the gas, the oil and of course the water. That means inroads into the rights of private property, in other words tasks of the socialist revolution. Equally, radical democracy at a national level cannot be achieved other than by breaking the grip of the oligarchy who ensure their control of the political process by corruption and violence. Democratic questions are directly interlinked with the issue of working class power.

The same considerations directly relate to the land struggle. The advent of (often US-controlled) agribusiness swivels the enemy from being simply local landlords, a subsector of the domestic bourgeoisie, to directly a struggle against transnational capitalist corporations. The fight against imperialism is one and the same as the struggle against the local oligarchy.

Revolutionary subject

The enormous growth of the cities, the development of agribusiness and semi-industrialisation in the major countries has significantly changed the revolutionary subject. This is summed up in the governmental slogan of nearly all of the Mexican militant left – "un gobierno obrero, campesino, indigena y popular"; a workers, peasants, indigenous and popular government. This crystallises what we can expect a revolutionary alliance in most of Latin America to be like.

Since the formulation of the 'workers and peasants government' formula in the 1920s, the growth of the informal sector in the cities, the barrio or favela dwellers, has been dramatic. Most of the urban poor are not regularly employed, but get by through street trading, small businesses, crime etc. The urban poor are a vital part of the base of the Bolivarian movement in Venezuela and of course of the mass movement which eventually brought Evo Morales and the MAS to power in Bolivia. The key demands of these people revolve around the basic questions of the provision of the basics of life – clean water, proper housing, sanitation, education and of course freedom from the violence and paternalistic manipulation by the state – ie democracy.

A new and positive feature of the Latin American movement has been the emergence of indigenous movements, the most well-known example being the Zapatistas in Mexico and sections of the movement in Bolivia. However there is a difference between the indigenous movement in those two countries. Subcommandante Marcos and the Zapatistas pose the solution to the demands of the indigenous people as being part of a transformation of Mexico nationwide, which Marcos tends to pose as 'democratisation" (not socialism).

Felipe Quispe ('El Mallku'), key leader of the indigenous people of El Alto in Bolivia, tends to project an Andean indigenous federation which might involve succession from existing Latin American countries. In Quispe's case, this idea sits in contradictory unity with his ideas about working class power in Bolivia.

One central feature cannot be avoided by the Latin American left – machismo and its opposite, women's liberation. While the leaders of the social movements in the barrios are disproportionately women, the violence against and super-exploitation of women on the most machismo of continents is incredible; from the daily subjugation of women as the most exploited workers in an often suffocating paternalistic family, to the ghastly mass murder of women in Guatemala. A more stable integration of women's liberation into the strategy of the Latin American left would unleash tremendous new forces and energies into the struggle.

The Question of Power

For the left, the decisive issue is how to integrate all these questions – of democracy, land reform, the destruction of the oligarchy, an end to economic robbery of the elite and imperialism, the basics of life for the urban poor and liberation for indigenous people and women – into a coherent overarching strategy for the popular masses to conquer power. The 'centre-left' – forces like the PT in Brazil, the Frente Amplio in Uruguay and the PRD of Manuel Lopez Obrador in Mexico – do not of course agree with this way of posing the question. For them it is about getting more justice within the system, and we have seen what this means in Uruguay and Brazil – abject capitulation to neoliberalism.

This poses a first question and problem – that of class independence, creating political parties of the popular masses, led politically by the working class, independent of bourgeois nationalist and populist forces. Building a broad class struggle party on a national basis is a task which Subcommandante Marcos and the Zapatistas have avoided confronting. However, the 'Other

Campaign' – a bold and audacious attempt to move out of their Chiapas mountain redoubts and unify the Mexican social movements indicates a renewed strategic thinking which – objectively – points in the direction of a new 'party' of the oppressed. How far this will go has yet to be seen.

The need for a strategy of conquering power, linked to that of class independence, is shown by the events between 2001 and 2004 in Argentina. Here a mass uprising overthrew the de la Rua government in December 2001, unleashing a political crisis which saw huge sections of the poor and the middle classes mobilised in self-organised action committees and picateros for more than a year.

But eventually this pre-revolutionary movement just petered out, precisely because there was no mass militant socialist party, capable of melding the rebellious forces in a coherent revolutionary national direction. As James Petras' excellent dissection of the Argentinian debacle points outpoints out:

"What clearly was lacking was a unified political organization (party, movement or combination of both) with roots in the popular neighborhoods which was capable of creating representative organs to promote class-consciousness and point toward taking state power. As massive and sustained as was the initial rebellious period (December2001-July 2002) no such political party or movement emerged – instead a multiplicity of localized groups with different agendas soon fell to quarreling over an elusive 'hegemony' – driving millions of possible supporters toward local face-to-face groups devoid of any political perspective."

The events in Argentina show the bankruptcy of the theory of refusing to take state power, an idea put forward by Subcommandante Marcos (and rendered more profound by the academic Jon Holloway). Refusing to challenge the bourgeoisie and the right wing for state power is linked to the refusal to build a workers political party. It leads, at best, to 'movementism from below', a continual opposition and protest, but with no idea of how to establish a global alternative and how to break the right, the oligarchy and their grip on state power.

How does the idea of the popular masses taking state power shape up to developments in Venezuela and Bolivia? In Venezuela the bourgeoisie have lost, or partially lost, control of the government but are still the economically ruling class – linked parasitically to the nationalised oil industry.

On the other hand, there is a tremendous development of popular self-organisation from below in the barrios and in the countryside; in addition substantial social progress has been made through the social 'missions', funded by oil revenues. However the poor remain legion in Venezuela and the solution to their problems will not be found outside of a radical redistribution of wealth, which means breaking the power and wealth of the oligarchy.

But in the context of a tremendous political polarisation in which the whole of the bourgeoisie and a big majority of the middle classes are against Chávez, this unstable equilibrium between the bourgeoisie and the masses, mediated by Chávez, cannot continue for ever. Sooner or later there will be a gigantic confrontation and the Bolivarian movement, and the Chávez leadership will have to make a choice. Depending on the loyalty of key army officers is useless.

With the threats of the right and imperialism the consolidation of popular committees into a national network of popular power is crucial. This must involve the arming of the popular sectors and the building of a popular militia.

There are important signs that polarisation is deepening rapidly. In Merida, right-wing students have organised prolonged riots. The recent national congress of the progressive union federation, the UNT, split between left and right and did not conclude its business or elect a new leadership. These are straws in the wind and it would be stupid to ignore the gathering storm clouds. Imperialism and the bourgeoisie want Chávez out, and there is now a race between revolution and counter-revolution. In Bolivia Evo Morales has moved decisively to clip the wings of the multinational corporations by nationalising the oil and gas. But this does not amount to expropriation, but in effect a significant hike in the taxes Bolivia charges the corporations. Even so his move is massively unpopular with imperialism and the right.

The exact direction in which the Morales government will go is unknown. In the medium term, Morales and his team will have to make their choice – between the oligarchy and imperialism on the one hand and the self-organised masses on the other. The example of Lula and the fate of the Brazilian PT is eloquent. If you try to avoid the question of power, you will end up either defeated or capitulating.

* Published by *International Viewpoint* online magazine : IV no 379, June 2006.

www.ingramcontent.com/pod-product-compliance
Lightning Source LLC
Chambersburg PA
CBHW021831020426
42334CB00014B/582